# A Season of

# Nature Poems for

# Catholic Children

---

## Spring

---

# A Spring Season of Nature Poems for Catholic Children

JANET P. MCKENZIE, OCDS

A RACE FOR HEAVEN BOOK

BIBLIO RESOURCE PUBLICATIONS, INC.
108½ S. MOORE ST.
BESSEMER, MI 49911
2020

Printed in the United States of America

## OTHER BOOKS IN THE NATURE POEMS FOR CATHOLIC CHILDREN SERIES

*A Summer Season of Nature Poems
for Catholic Children*

*An Autumn Season of Nature Poems
for Catholic Children*

*A Winter Season of Nature Poems
for Catholic Children*

# OTHER BOOKS BY JANET P. MCKENZIE

## WWW.RACEFORHEAVEN.COM

### STUDY GUIDES AND AIDS

✟ A Series of 20 Saint Study Guides for the saint books written by Mary Fabyan Windeatt (available as individual study guides or grade-level guides)

✟ *Graced Encounters with Mary Fabyan Windeatt's Saints: 344 Ways to Imitate the Holy Habits of Saints*

✟ *The Windeatt Dictionary: Pre-Vatican II Terms and Catholic Words from Mary Fabyan Windeatt's Saint Biographies*

✟ *Reading the Saints: Lists of Catholic Books for Children plus Book Collecting Tips for the Home and School Library, Second Edition*

✟ *Alternative Books Reports for Catholic Students*

✟ *The King of the Golden City Study Edition* (includes text and guide or individual guide available)

✟ *Outlaws of Ravenhurst Study Edition* (includes text and guide or individual guide available)

✟ *The Family that Overtook Christ Study Edition: Lessons in Sanctity from the Family of St. Bernard of Clairvaux* (includes text and guide)

✟ *By Cross and Anchor Study Edition: The Story of Frederic Baraga on Lake Superior* (includes text and guide)

### RECONCILIATION/FIRST HOLY COMMUNION

✟ *A Reconciliation Reader-Retreat: Read-aloud Lessons, Stories, and Poems for Young Catholics Preparing for Confession*

✟ *Communion with the Saints, A Family Preparation Program for First Communion and Beyond in the Spirit of St. Therese*

✟ *The King of the Golden City Study Edition* (includes text and guide or individual guide available)

✟ *My First Communion Journal in Imitation of St. Therese, the Little Flower*

✟ *My First Communion Journal in Imitation of St. Paul: Putting on the Armor of God*

✟ *The Good Shepherd and His Little Lambs Study Edition: A First Communion Story-Primer*

## SACRAMENT OF CONFIRMATION

✟ *A Confirmation Reader-Retreat: Read-Aloud Lessons, Stories, and Poems for Young Catholics*

✟ *The Family that Overtook Christ Study Edition: Lessons in Sanctity from the Family of St. Bernard of Clairvaux* (adult and teens)

## ST. JOSEPH

✟ *The Month of St. Joseph: Prayers and Practices for Each Day of March in Imitation of the Virtues of St. Joseph* (adult)

✟ *Devotion to St. Joseph: Read-Aloud Stories, Poems, and Prayers for Catholic Children*

## OTHER BOOKS

✟ *I Talk with God: The Art of Prayer and Meditation for Catholic Children*

✟ *Bedtime Bible Stories for Catholic Children: Loving Jesus through His Word*

THIS BOOK IS DEDICATED TO MY GRANDCHILDREN:
ALI, GRACE, NORAH, ETHAN, KATIE, JON, JACOB,
ELENA, AND ALL THOSE TO COME.

NATURE IS SO MUCH MORE FUN AND INSPIRING
WHEN I EXPLORE IT WITH YOU.

WITH GREAT LOVE,
NANA

# ACKNOWLEDGEMENTS

Dust Jacket Design by Joshua Kodis

Dust Jacket Photo ©yuelan iStockPhoto.com

Dust Jacket Graphics ©Peter Snow
iStockPhoto.com

Divider Page Illustration ©geraria iStockPhoto.com

March 4 Illustration ©NataLima
Shutterstock.com

March 24 Illustration ©Nadia 80
Shutterstock.com

March 27 and April 26 Illustrations ©Hein Nouwens
Shutterstock.com

April 10 Illustration ©Morphart Creation
Shutterstock.com

May 6 Illustration ©Channarong Pherngjanda
Shutterstock.com

May 9 Illustration ©grzhmelek Shutterstock.com

May 25 Illustration ©Bodor Tivadar ShutterStock.com

"To the Immaculate Heart of Mary"
© 2019 Janet P. McKenzie

But now ask the beasts to teach you,
the birds of the air to tell you;
Or speak to the earth to instruct you,
and the fish of the sea to inform you.
Which of all these does not know
that the hand of God has done this?

Job 12:7-9

And Nature, the old nurse, took
The child upon her knee,
Saying: "Here is a story-book
thy Father has written for thee."

"Come, wander with me," she said,
"Into regions yet untrod;
And read what is still unread
In the manuscripts of God."

And he wandered away and away
With Nature, the dear old nurse,
Who sang to him night and day
The rhymes of the universe.

From "The Fiftieth Birthday of Agassiz" by
Henry Wadsworth Longfellow (1807-1882)

# TABLE OF CONTENTS

# PREFACE

Throughout my childhood, my father worked as a manager in the Michigan State Parks system. We moved every three or four years to a different park within Michigan's Upper Peninsula. Even as a young child, I remember spending long days and evenings outdoors—in the woods, on the beach, in the yard. Many of these memories include my siblings and neighborhood friends. But many are the times I spent alone at various "secret" places I had found, places I often escaped to in order to think deep-child thoughts—to communicate with God.

Although I hesitate to compare my experiences with those of a saint, St. Thérèse the Little Flower, describes similar experiences in *The Story of a Soul*: "I preferred to go *alone* and sit down on the grass bedecked with flowers, and then my thoughts became very profound indeed! Without knowing what it was to meditate, my soul was absorbed in real prayer" (SOS 37). St. Thérèse talks often of how she was inspired to love, praise, and understand the God that the book of nature opened to her.

As a Discalced Carmelite Secular, my life is focused on union with God. Like St. Augustine (yes, another saint comparison!), I searched for many years for God, in various places and circumstances. However, in my Carmelite journey of faith, I have discovered that God can be found within. He resides in our very souls—nearer to us than we are to ourselves. Yet, in my adult searching, I have found—just as in my childhood—that I often commune best with Him in natural environments. I feel His presence in the beauty and holy silence of nature. Surrounded by creation, my mind frees, my soul fills with gratitude, and my heart connects with our loving Creator.

Here too we are in good company with the saints. Both St. Teresa of Jesus and St. John of the Cross, Carmelite Doctors, often used the natural world as a conduit to God:

✝ "It helped me also to look at fields, or water, or flowers. In these things I found a remembrance of the creator. I mean that they awakened and recollected me and served as a book and reminded me of my ingratitude and sins" (St. Teresa of Jesus, *Life* 9.5).

✝ "Beholding in creation a trace of the divine beauty, power, and loving wisdom, John could not easily resist the enchantment of nature. . . . He would take the friars out to the mountains . . . so that each might pass the day alone there 'in solitary prayer'" (*The Collected Works of St. John of the Cross* 26).

Many are the quotations we could cite from saints, popes, theologians, the Catechism, and Scripture that support an appreciation of the natural world as an important dimension of our relationship with God. However, we also need an awareness of the errors of the "New Age" movement, the theological problems with "nature worship", the heresy of pantheism, and an understanding that God does not depend upon creation for His identity to direct our path. If you are concerned or curious about these issues, please review the Appendix of this book.

In this series, we embark upon a study of nature and God in nature by reading aloud one poem per day, spending time daily outdoors, and, like St. Thérèse, thinking about God. I believe that the beauty, the rhythm, the flow, and the openness of poetry lends itself particularly useful as we journey closer to God with our beloved children and grandchildren in union with what Pope Frances calls "the joyful mystery of God" in creation. May God bless you!

16 July, 2019, Feast of Our Lady of Mount Carmel

# A Few Explanations and Suggestions
## The Purpose of This Study

The purpose of this poetical study of nature through the seasons is two-fold:

1) To seek and experience God personally and intimately by daily exposure to His creative work in nature

2) To better appreciate the connection between all of God's creation, its meaning and value, and its role—and ours—in the harmonious praise of God

Briefly, each creation of God has its own value and significance as well as a unique nature that is dependent on the rest of creation. Each creature works to complete and serve the rest of creation. (See *CCC* ¶340.) All of creation's natures, working together as a system of natures, are what we call "nature"—which "can only be understood as a gift from the outstretched hand of the Father of all" (*Laudato Si'* ¶76). The purpose of all of God's creation—including us—is to give Him praise and glory: ". . . so that we might exist for the praise of his glory . . ." (Ephesians 1:12).

Our study of God's creation through poetry and outdoor exploration is intended to allow children—and their adult companions—to experience God in a different way, to see Him in a new light, and to deepen our relationship and appreciation for Him and all of His creation—to learn to pray and praise God continuously. This is not a new way of experiencing God. Check out the Psalms and other books of the Bible. Refer to the writings of St. Thomas

Aquinas and many other saints. Peruse the teachings of our last three popes—St. Pope John Paul II, Pope Benedict XVI, and Pope Francis. Read through the *Catechism of the Catholic Church*, which clearly states: "There is a solidarity among all creatures arising from the fact that all have the same Creator and are all ordered to his glory . . ." (344). (For a more thorough treatment of seeking God through nature in accordance with the teachings of the Catholic Church, please see the Appendix of this book.)

Hopefully, through the gentle art of poetry and a daily commitment to experience God's creation outdoors, our relationship with God will become more awestruck as it becomes filled with the wonder, love, and appreciation of His divine wisdom and loving providence. God is more than willing to meet us whenever we reach out to Him. A little bit of openness and availability on our part will go a long way toward helping us fulfill our mission to praise God's glory in all our being. Let us begin today.

## HOW THIS STUDY IS ORGANIZED

### ASTRONOMICAL VS. METEOROLOGICAL SEASONS

Astronomical seasons are based on where the sun is in relation to the Earth, with the equinoxes (March and September) marking the dates where the day-to-night ratio is exactly twelve hours each. Because the Earth does not take exactly 365 days to travel around the sun, these dates vary but are generally considered to be March 21 and September 22 with the solstices usually falling on June 21 and December 22—the days with the longest and shortest periods of daylight. So the first day of each season according to the astronomical calendar would correspond to the varying dates of the spring and fall equinoxes and the summer and winter solstices.

The meteorological calendar for seasons uses the more general three-month chunk of time that is most closely associated with that season's weather. This calendar has the following seasonal dates:

- Winter: December 1 to February 28 or 29
- Spring: March 1 to May 31
- Summer: June 1 to August 31, and
- Autumn: September 1 to November 30

As the meteorological seasonal calendar corresponds more closely with our liturgical year, which begins in the season of Advent around December 1, (and breaks the months of each season more cleanly), this poetical study of the seasons uses the meteorological calendar to track the seasons.

(Please note that much of the material in this study is geared toward the weather and activities common to the temperate climates. My personal experience is almost exclusively that of the upper Midwest of the United States. Adaptation may be necessary depending on your location.)

## LITURGICAL VS. NATURAL YEAR

Traditionally, we Americans often begin new projects and make new resolutions at the beginning of our Gregorian calendar year on January 1. Our Church's Roman Rite liturgical new year always begins on the first Sunday of Advent. This date is determined by when the Sunday closest to the Feast of St. Andrew (November 30) falls. The earliest this date can be is November 27, and the latest possible date is December 3. The beginning of the winter season of this series would roughly correspond with the beginning of the Church's liturgical new year.

The other major season of the liturgical year is the season of Lent, which is generally associated with the natural

3

season of spring. As the timing of this season depends on the moveable feast day of Easter, Ash Wednesday, the first day of Lent, may be as early as February 4 or as late as March 10, with the date of Easter itself ranging from March 22 to April 25. Therefore, the Lenten season is covered in this study in both the winter and spring seasons.

## WHEN AND HOW TO START

There is no "right" starting place for this series—no "correct" season to begin this poetical study of God's creation. Many may wish to start with the Church's new liturgical year in December—the winter season. However, feel free to start with the season that best suits your own calendar and availability. Perhaps summer, when school is in recess and life is more laid back, is a better fit for your schedule. Quite possibly, autumn—the beginning of the school year—appeals to you as the best time to start. Maybe you want to examine the optional theme for each season and choose to begin according to which theme seems most interesting to you and your family.

Whenever you begin, remember the program's two main rules:
1. Read one poem daily *aloud* and have a short discussion on it. (Suggestions for age-appropriate questions can be found below.)
2. Spend at least thirty minutes each and every day outdoors, exploring God's beautiful creative work. This includes you as well as the children. Always keep in mind that the best way to get children outdoors is to go with them. Trust me; you will be enriched beyond your expectations. Do not hesitate to assume the role of nature mentor to help

your children or grandchildren increase their love of nature and deepen their experience of God. Review the section on nature mentoring if you need the reassurance that no prior experience or knowledge is necessary. You—yes, you—can do this!

## THE DAILY ROUTINE

### THE POEMS – DAILY AND SUPPLEMENTAL

For each day of the year, a poem (or several shorter poems) is presented for reading. The poem may be about an aspect of nature for that season, relate to the seasonal theme, or to a specific activity common for that season. Read each poem aloud. Perhaps each child could also read the poem aloud. Read slowly and with feeling. Don't hesitate to re-read the poem several times. If a child takes a special liking to a poem, help the child to memorize it. Having three or four favorite poems in a memory bank provides a store of great pleasure that will bubble up and spill out on days when our love of nature overwhelms us and we have no other way to express our joy in that special experience. It is a great treasure.

In addition to the daily poems, several other poems are available in the supplemental poetry section following the daily poems. These poems focus on the liturgical year or specific national holidays. They may be chosen to read aloud instead of, or in addition to, the poem for each day. There is a poem available for each day of Christmas, each day of Lent, and at least one poem for each significant holiday or Catholic holy day. Additionally, there are poems for meditation upon the themes for the First Friday and First Saturday devotions. Use the supplemental poems as you deem best for your family—either replacing the daily poem, read in addition to the daily poem, or not read at all. If you wish to incorporate them into the daily routine, it may require some preparation time to preview these poems to determine which ones best suit your family and purposes. Be sure to discuss these poems with the children/grandchildren just as you would the daily poems.

As you and your family begin to read more and more poetry, be sure to note favorite poets. Go online and check out more poems by these favorites or perhaps purchase as a gift an entire volume written by them. Pay attention to the type of poetry (rhythm and rhyme scheme) that appeals to each child. Encourage them to take a favorite poem, study how it is written, and use it as a pattern for writing an original poem of their own. Perhaps after reading a poem, they may decide that they could write a better poem on that topic. The world needs poetry and poets; coax the young poets around you to produce poetry that they enjoy writing and sharing. Model writing poetry by generating poems of your own.

## DISCUSSION

To encourage discussion, always ask open-ended questions that require more than a yes/no answer. For younger children, the following questions offer a good beginning but remember that not all questions will apply to every poem. As you gain confidence, feel free to construct your own questions geared toward the ages and interests of your own children/grandchildren.

1. What is this poem about?
2. How does this poem make you feel?
3. What action do you want to take because of this poem?
4. What did you learn from this poem?
3. What does this poem suggest about God?

A different approach is to ask each child to retell the poem in their own words, starting with the youngest child and having each child add something to the re-telling. (Educator Charlotte Mason calls this technique "narration.")

For older children (and adults), try using the following three principles/realities/values that stem from the teachings of Thomas Berry, Catholic eco-theologian and author of several books including *The Dream of the Earth* and *The Great Work: Our Way into the Future*. According to Thomas Berry, these three characteristics govern the universe and reveal what the universe has to teach us. (These questions are also appropriate to ask as a nature mentor when outside exploring nature with children.)

1. Uniqueness (Each creation offers a unique expression of the divine, an authenticity that illustrates how the divine image dwells within.)
   - How is this creation different from all others? What makes it unique?
   - How does it reveal the divine?

2. Interior Identity
   - What is the job or specific task of this creation?
   - How does it function?
   - How does it give harmonious praise to God?

3. Communion/Connection
   - What is the relationship between this creation and the rest of creation?
   - How does it serve or provide for the rest of creation?
   - How is it connected to or dependent upon the rest of creation?

## THE QUOTATIONS

The quotations beneath the daily poems are included for the adults participating in this study. Often, as we feed our children the knowledge and inspiration they crave and need, our own needs may go unfulfilled. These short selections are intended to inspire you, deepen your understanding about an idea or topic, or add a touch of humor.

## ADDITIONAL RESOURCES

This section first includes appropriate picture books for children. In preparation for this section, hundreds of possibly worthy picture books were read and examined; many of these books were discarded in favor of the exceptional books chosen for each season. The books marked "Stellar" would be considered "must reads" for each season. The remaining books have been categorized according to the holidays and optional themes for each season. The intention is that these books would be read aloud by either an adult or child.

Depending on the interests of your children/grandchildren, you may wish to focus on one particular theme or perhaps choose several books from each category. (It would be hard to read them all!) As you read through these books, be sure to note the author of those books you particularly enjoy. Watch for other books by these authors listed in this series, and/or check them out at your local library.

After the final section of picture books, there is a short section on other nature books for children. This section varies with the season and is outlined below.

Spring: A Short List of Children's Nature Authors
Summer: A Short List of Children's Nature Poets, Collectable Children's Poetry Books, and A Few Children's Poetry Anthologies

Fall: A Short List of Children's Nature Chapter Books
Winter: Nature Non-fiction Books for Children

The last part of this section contains recommended adult books that fall loosely in the following categories:
- The "Why" of Nature
- Connection with Nature
- Nature Activity Books—Outdoor Adventuring
- Nature Journaling
- Nature Crafts and Drawing Books
- Nature Books for Grandparents
- The Practice of *Shinrin-yoku:* Forest Therapy or Forest Bathing
- The Practice of Mindfulness

## OUTSIDE ACTIVITY

The crux and primary purpose of this poetry series is to explore nature and to seek God in His beautiful creation. If you are unsure about what to do outside, check out the "Additional Resources" section described above for ideas. Assume your role as nature mentor as described on pages 17-21 below.

By spending unfettered time in nature, we will unleash our sense of wonder and come to better understand God. By increasing our familiarity with different aspects of nature, we will begin to see the connection between all creation and discover the loving concern God has for His creation.

Please make the effort to get your family (including yourself!) outside for least thirty minutes each day—an hour would not be too much! Get outside, play, experience creation, and live in the present moment. Be sure to pause occasionally in holy silence to give thanks, glory, and praise to our awesome Creator!

## OPTIONAL SEASONAL THEMES

For those interested in a more guided study of nature, each season has a theme of recommended focus. These themes provide a hub around which outside activity for each season can be centered as well as an emphasis on specific knowledge and experience of God's created world.

Do not get obsessive with the suggested resources below. Choose only those best suited to your particular situation. Be flexible. Taylor these suggestions to your own circumstances and time allowances.

SPRING THEME: Detecting God in Nature through Phenology

- DEFINITION OF PHENOLOGY: Nature's calendar; nature's clock; the study of the timing of seasonal biological activities including first flowers, leaf budding, bird migration, etc. (We can also include *seasonality*, which is the study of changes in the physical environment such as first frost, date the ice melts, etc.)

- GOAL: Nature Detective—someone who carefully observes the wonders and mystery of nature

- SUMMARY: Spend spring observing firsts and lasts in nature: first robin, first eruptions of various plants and flowers, first sound of the frog voices, last frost, last ice on the lake. Mark these dates on a regular or perpetual calendar—an excellent beginning toward keeping a more complete nature journal. Allow the children free rein to explore and take notes and photos of various aspects of God's creation. "Nature is a constant source of wonder and awe" (Pope Francis, *Laudato Si'* 85).

# A Few Explanations and Suggestions

- ADULT RESOURCES
  - Daily readings from any of the following: *Hal Borland's Book of Days* (New England), *A Walk through the Year* by Edwin Way Teale (New England), or *Wit & Wisdom of the Great Outdoors* by Larry Wilber (upper Midwest)
  - **Or** weekly readings from *The Beginning Naturalist* by Gale Lawrence or shorter articles for each month in *A Seasonal Guide to the Natural Year* by John Bates (upper Midwest), or *Minnesota Phenology* by Larry Weber
  - **Or** browse through any calendar/almanac suited to your location.
  - Check into joining a citizen science program of interest.

- CHILDREN'S RESOURCES
  - *Crinkleroot's Nature Almanac* by Jim Arnosky
  - *One Day in the Woods* by Jean Craighead George
  - *This World of Wonder* by Hal Borland
  - *When I Consider* by Marian M. Schoolland

SUMMER THEME: Inspecting God's Glorious Creation through Naming Nature (Nomenclature)

- DEFINITION OF NOMENCLATURE: A system of names in a given field such as botany or biology

- GOAL: Naturalist—someone who is an expert or student in the study of plants, animals, and the natural world

- SUMMARY: By taking an interest in nature and being willing to make the acquaintance of the most common natural elements in your locale—by learning the names of the most common birds, flowers,

11

and trees—we can become more acquainted with all that surrounds us in God's great outdoors. Names foster familiarity, and lead to a sense of connection. "What I know of the divine sciences and the Holy Scriptures, I have learned in woods and fields. I have no other masters than the beeches and the oaks" (St. Bernard of Clairvaux).

- ADULT RESOURCES
  - 📖 *Beyond Your Doorstep* by Hal Borland
  - 📖 *Circle of the Seasons* by Edwin Way Teale
  - 📖 *Exploring Nature with Your Child* by Dorothy Edwards Shuttlesworth
  - 📖 *Great Lakes Nature* by Mary Blocksma
  - 📖 *Handbook of Nature Study* by Anna Botsford Comstock [a classic since 1939]
  - 📖 *The Naturalist's Notebook* by Nathaniel T. Wheelwright and Bernd Heinrich

- CHILDREN'S RESOURCES
  - 📖 Regional field guides (the more specific to your area the better) to birds, flowers, insects, trees, or any other area of interest
  - 📖 *Nature Anatomy* by Julia Rothman
  - 📖 Any of the *True Books* (*True Book of Insects*, etc.) published by Children's Press in the 1950's and 1960's
  - 📖 Any of Jim Arnosky's *Crinkleroot's Guide to Knowing* books (*Birds*, *Trees*, etc.)
  - 📖 *Crinkleroot's Guide to Walking in Wild Places*

AUTUMN THEME: Respecting God's Creation through Care of the Natural World

- GOAL: Eco-Catholic

- DEFINITION OF ECO-CATHOLIC: Someone who values not only Catholic spirituality and doctrine but also the natural world, the environment, and justice

- SUMMARY: In his 2015 encyclical *Laudato Si'*, Pope Francis encourages "every person living on this planet" to take better care of our common home, Earth. Like his three predecessors, he emphasizes the need to care for and understand the connection between all of God's creation. Review carefully your family's relationship with the natural world and the habits that support the environment and those that are detrimental. "Care for the environment represents a challenge for all of humanity. It is a matter of a common and universal duty, that of respecting a common good" (Pope St. John Paul II, *Centesimus Annus*, 40).

- ADULT RESOURCES
  - *Caring for Creation in Your Own Backyard: Over 100 Things Christian Families Can Do to Help the Earth (A Seasonal Guide)* by Loren & Mary Ruth Wilkinson
  - *Earthsongs: Praying with Nature* by Wayne Simsic
  - *In Defense of Nature* by Benjamin Wiker
  - *Laudato Si'* by Pope Francis
  - *Life from Our Land* by Marcus Grodi
  - *The Joyful Mystery: Field Notes toward a Green Thomism* by Christopher J. Thompson

- CHILDREN'S RESOURCES
  - *Celebrate the Earth: Psalm 104* by Dorrie Papademetriou
  - *Crinkleroot's Guide to Giving Back to Nature* by Jim Arnosky

📖 *Song of Francis* by Tomie dePaola
📖 Read and implement actions proposed by Pope Francis in ¶211 of *Laudato Si'*.

WINTER THEME: Reflecting on the Mystery of God through Natural Prayer

- DEFINITION OF NATURAL PRAYER: Finding intimacy with God by experiencing Him in the beauty of nature; prayer experienced amidst creation (Beware, however, of the caution expressed by St. John of the Cross in *Ascent of Mount Carmel* 3.24.4: If the heart and soul are not elevated to God, an experience of sensory delight may merely be another form of recreation.)

- GOAL: Mystic—someone who seeks union with God through prayer and self-surrender

- SUMMARY: The season of winter—when much of nature is at rest and we anticipate and contemplate the Mystery of God in the Christ Child—is a great time to reconnect with that wonder for God that natural experiences (a beautiful sunset, a snowy-topped mountain, a perfect snowflake) so easily enkindle. Enjoy the stillness of winter while practicing the virtue of holy silence—quiet walks in the snow, a pause to listen to the winter birds. Take your daily prayer time (rosary or meditation) outside. "We need to find God, and he cannot be found in noise and restlessness. God is the friend of silence. See how nature—trees, flowers, grass—grows in silence; see the stars, the moon and the sun, how they move in silence . . ." (St. Teresa of Calcutta).

- ADULT RESOURCES
  - 📖 *Natural Prayer: Encountering God in Nature* by Wayne Simsic
  - 📖 *The Secret Life of John Paul II* by Lino Zani
  - 📖 *When the Trees Say Nothing* by Thomas Merton
- CHILDREN'S RESOURCES
  - 📖 *A Quiet Place* by Douglas Wood
  - 📖 *Crinkleroot's Book of Animal Tracking* by Jim Arnosky
  - 📖 *The Other Way to Listen* by Byrd Baylor
  - 📖 *The Wild Weather Book* by Fiona Danks and Jo Schofield
  - 📖 *WoodsWalk* by Henry W. Art and Michael W. Robbins

---

Note that these suggested themes are *optional*. If the children are young, or if the themes seem intimidating to implement, feel free to skip them. Perhaps you would like to utilize the picture books as your only use of the optional season themes. Or maybe you would like to study the suggested adult resources for your own enrichment without adding the children's resources.

Be kind to yourself. We're going for joy here—not added stress! Do not put pressure to use every resource and/or theme. Attach no guilt to customizing and simplifying. The main objective is to enjoy God's creation and to connect with the Creator—not to cram in every possible teaching moment. Allow the children to ask and find answers to their own spontaneous questions in an adventure of discovery at their own lead. Relax and enjoy!

"FOR FROM THE GREATNESS
AND THE BEAUTY OF CREATED THINGS
THEIR ORIGINAL AUTHOR,
BY ANALOGY,
IS SEEN."

WISDOM 13:5

# YOU CAN BECOME A NATURE MENTOR (ALMOST WITHOUT TRYING)

"If a child is to keep alive his inborn sense of wonder . . . he needs the companionship of at least one adult who can share it, rediscovering with him the joy, excitement, and mystery of the world we live in" (Rachel Carson in *A Sense of Wonder*). This "one adult" becomes this child's nature mentor. It is not a difficult task. It does not require vast knowledge. According to Rachel Carson, it is based upon "having fun together rather than teaching." Whether you are a grandparent, a parent, a teacher, the neighbor down the street, or an aunt like Rachel Carson, you need no advance preparation other than asking yourself, "Am I up for adventure?" "Can I handle being a co-conspirator?"

The best nature mentors are not those who have the answers but who can stimulate the questions, who can step aside and let the child take charge. Effective nature mentors are those who are fellow adventurers, willing to let their own sense of wonder come alive, and share their feelings about nature—and reverence for nature—rather than merely providing explanations and facts. Observe and explore. Be aware and listen—not only to the wonders around you but to those sharing the experience with you. Be respectful to the child's interests and enthusiasms. Be attentive to the present moment—the activity and the feelings that are evoked.

Ask questions. Point out interesting sights, sounds, animals, and plants. Bring home specimens to talk about, learn about, and display. Include God in the discussion.

Help them to observe the activity around them. Allow them to directly experience the wonder that surrounds them —saving the "teaching moment" for a later recap of the event. Encourage them to see, hear, smell, and touch. Allow them not only to run and enjoy but also to sit in holy silence and observe—watch the grass bending in the wind, hear the babble of nearby water and birds, smell the flowers and the bark of the trees, touch the moss and slippery rocks—pondering and raising the heart to God. The love of nature is best inspired by experiencing nature —even quiet observation can be an interactive encounter on an emotional level.

Be enthusiastic and joyful in all their discoveries. Play games; join in their fun. Often, the memory of an experience is associated with the emotions related to that experience. By making time with nature joy-filled, joy will come to be an emotion associated with nature itself.

Sharing the natural world with others adds to the richness of the encounter—not only at the moment but later in discussion. Take time each day to reflect together on time spent in nature, reviewing individual discoveries and emotions. In this way, everyone benefits from each person's experience and insights, and our own encounters become more meaningful. Additionally, a bit of nature bonding and affirmation occurs that binds us with each other, and more deeply with the created world.

As a nature mentor, basic knowledge may be helpful but, in this case, only a little knowledge of nature is not a dangerous thing—or even detrimental. Enjoyment of simple natural aspects (the colors of the sunset, the blowing clouds, the calls of birds, the vastness of the night sky, the feel of rain on your face) will serve to enkindle more joy and wonder than many interesting facts. "I sincerely believe that for the child, and for the parent seeking to guide him, it is not half so important to know as to feel" (Rachel Carson).

It is more helpful to arouse their curiosity and sense of wonder than to pepper them with facts and names they may or may not be able to assimilate. As a nature mentor, receptivity and awareness trump personal resources. Is it less wondrous to gaze at the night sky even if you do not know the name of a single star or constellation?

Encourage exploration using the senses of smell and hearing. This is particularly effective at night and in rainy weather. The smell of the ocean, frog ponds, and rain-filled forests can provide lasting memories. The night sound of insects, frogs, flight of birds overhead, thunder, and wind are especially powerful. Try to focus not only on the full chorus of sound but also on each of the individual contributors. Seek where they are hiding.

Unfortunately, it is easy to become immune to the wonder of God's creation—to become insensitive to repeated exposure to God's great gifts. Rachel Carson would have us ask, "What if I had never seen this before? What if I knew I would never see it again?" Like the reception of Holy Communion, when we take for granted that we can receive It often, we often receive It less (and less reverently). The same holds true of God's gifts within the natural world. Because we can see it all the time, we often see (and enjoy its benefits) less often. When is the last time you took the time to explore the night sky? Or pause your busy agenda to enjoy the glorious sunset? Or listen attentively for even a minute or two to the morning chorus of birds? Learn to tune in to God not only in church, but also in His cathedral of the natural world.

## RESOURCES

So what resources are required to be an effective nature mentor? For starters, you may want to read one or more of the books that most directly influenced the above insights and ideas:

&#x1F4D5; *The Sense of Wonder* by Rachel Carson (1956)

&#x1F4D5; *Sharing Nature with Children: The Classic Parents' and Teachers' Nature Awareness Guidebook* by Joseph Cornell (1979—a newer edition is available)

&#x1F4D5; *How to Raise a Wild Child: The Art and Science of Falling in Love with Nature* by Scott D. Sampson (2015)

Spending a few dollars on a good magnifying glass or hands lens will pay off handsomely. With this, a snowflake or grain of sand takes on far greater wonder as does a drop of pond water or the moon at night. You may wish to throw down another couple of dollars on child-sized flashlights—or ultraviolet flashlights!—for night exploration of insects, rocks, and flowers. (Bedtime can wait!)

As far as expensive equipment and toys, do not let your heart be troubled. In 2012, *Wired* magazine published an article entitled "The 5 Best Toys of All Time." Here is your shopping list:

1. Stick

2. Box

3. String

4. Cardboard Tube

5. Dirt

If you must spend money, a few good field guides may be helpful—the more regional the better—for identification of common trees, birds, flowers, and insects. Keep in mind, however, this caution from Rachel Carson: "I think the value of the game of identification depends on how you play it. If it becomes an end in itself, I count it of little use. It is possible to compile extensive lists of creatures seen and identified without ever once having caught a breath-taking glimpse of the wonder of life. If a child asked me a question that suggested even a faint awareness of the mystery behind the arrival of a migrant sandpiper on the beach of an August morning, I would be far more pleased than by the mere fact that he knew it was a sandpiper and not a plover."

A pair of puddle boots, some old clothes, and raingear (purchased or makeshift) will allow your child to explore without fear of "getting dirty." Be sure to provide the same for yourself.

Nature mentoring really is as simple as accompanying kids outside and letting them do what comes naturally. Let them be the boss. If you are doubtful, try at least a half-hour outside every day for a month—put it on your calendar. While Scott Sampson in *How to Raise a Wild Child* claims, "The best place to fall in love with nature is wherever you happen to be," be sure to vary the setting occasionally. Find a place where you (as well as the children) are excited to be. See what effect this daily thirty-minute habit has—on you and the kids!

Rachel Carson had one wish for every child: ". . . a sense of wonder so indestructible that it would last throughout life, as an unfailing antidote against the boredom and disenchantments of later years, the sterile preoccupation with things that are artificial, the alienation from the sources of our strength." It is in wonder that we often find God.

"... HE FIXED THE ORDERED SEASONS
AND THE BOUNDARIES OF
THEIR REGIONS,
SO THAT PEOPLE MIGHT SEEK GOD,
EVEN PERHAPS GROPE FOR HIM
AND FIND HIM,
THOUGH INDEED HE IS NOT FAR
FROM ANY ONE OF US."

ACTS 17:26-27

# March

## To March

Emily Dickinson (1830-1886), published in *Poems*, 1922

Dear March, come in!
How glad I am!
I looked for you before.
Put down your hat
You must have walked
How out of breath you are!
Dear March, how are you?
And the rest?
Did you leave Nature well?
Oh, March, come right upstairs with me,
I have so much to tell!

I got your letter, and the birds';
The maples never knew
That you were coming, I declare,
How red their faces grew!
But, March, forgive me
And all those hills
You left for me to hue;
There was no purple suitable,
You took it all with you. . . .

"BUT NOW ASK THE BEASTS TO TEACH YOU,
THE BIRDS OF THE AIR TO TELL YOU; OR SPEAK
TO THE EARTH TO INSTRUCT YOU, AND THE
FISH OF THE SEA TO INFORM YOU."
JOB 12:7-8

## MARCH

Constance Fenimore Woolson (1840-1894),
published in *Child's Calendar Beautiful*, 1905

Galloping, galloping, galloping in,

Into the world with a stir and a din.
The north wind, the east wind, the west wind
together
In-bringing, in-bringing the March's wild
weather.

## SPRING

Daniel A. Lord (1888-1955), published in
*Chants for Children*, 1942

All happy and glad in the sunshine I stood.

For isn't spring lovely and isn't God good?

"It was one of those March days when the sun shines
hot, and the wind blows cold, when it is summer in the
light and winter in the shade." – Charles Dickens

## EASTER RHYME
Published in
*Our Little Tot's Speaker*, 1899

"Thirty days hath September,"
Every person can remember;
But to know when Easter comes
Puzzles even scholars some.

When March the twenty-first is past
Just watch the silvery moon,
And when you see it full and round,
Know Easter'll be here soon.

After the moon has reached its full,
Then Easter will be here,
The very Sunday after
In each and every year.

And if it hap on Sunday
The moon should reach its height,
The Sunday following this event
Will be the Easter bright.

"Within all of creation lies God, waiting to be
discovered." – Unknown

## THE WIND
Robert Louis Stevenson (1850-1894), published in
*A Child's Garden of Verses*, 1885

I saw you toss the kites on high
And blow the birds about the sky;
And all around I heard you pass,
Like ladies' skirts across the grass—
    O wind, a-blowing all day long,
    O wind, that sings so loud a song!

I saw the different things you did,
But always you yourself you hid.
I felt you push, I heard you call,
I could not see yourself at all—
    O wind, a-blowing all day long,
    O wind, that sings so loud a song.

O you, that are so strong and cold,
O blower, are you young or old?
Are you a beast of field and tree.
Or just a stronger child than me?
    O wind a blowing all day long,
    O wind that sings so loud a song!

"Climb the mountains and get their good tidings.
Nature's peace will flow into you as sunshine flows into
trees. The winds will blow their own freshness into you,
and the storms their energy, while cares will drop
away from you like the leaves of autumn." – John Muir

## I HEARD IT IN THE VALLEY
Annette Wynne (died 1953),
published in *Days and Days*, 1919

I heard it in the valley,
I heard it in the glen;
Listen, children, surely, surely,
Spring is coming back again!

I heard it in the valley,
I heard it on the hill,
I heard it where the bare trees stand,
Very brave and still.

I heard it in the valley,
I heard the waters start,
I heard it surely, surely,
I heard it in my heart!

"Everyone has a listening point somewhere, some
quiet place where he can contemplate the
awesome universe." – Sigurd Olson

## EAVESDROPPERS

Mary Carolyn Davies (1888-1940?), published in
*A Little Freckled Person*, 1919

The stars lean down and listen,

At fairy-story time;
They twinkle and they glisten
To hear each happy rhyme;
To all our cheerful singing
The little stars beat time.

The stars lean down and hear us,
They know it's not polite,
But then, they cease to fear us,
About this time of night.
They creep and edge up near us,
Although it isn't right.

Eavesdroppers! But we love them,
We leave a little space,
And never crowd or shove them,
Because, in any case,
That stretch of blue above them
Is such a lonely place!

"Myriads of stars were my net that night, but I no longer felt lonely, for I knew that while man might unravel the puzzled skein of life and solve the riddles of the universe, what really matters is the wonder which makes it all possible." – Sigurd Olson

## THE MOUNTAINS
Mary Carolyn Davies (1888-1940?), published in
*A Little Freckled Person*, 1919

The mountains do not stir, or show

Emotion when Spring comes, I know;
But though they are restrained by pride,
I think that they are glad inside!

## RAIN
Robert Louis Stevenson (1850-1894), published in
*A Child's Garden of Verses*, 1885

The rain is raining all around,

It falls on field and tree,
It rains on the umbrellas here,
And on the ships at sea.

"Ultimately, he [St. Pope John Paul II] and I always
knew that ascending the rocky flanks of a mountain is
a bit like walking in a holy place." – Leno Zani, *The
Secret Life of John Paul II*

## THE LITTLEST CLOUD

Mary Carolyn Davies (1888-1940?), published in
*A Little Freckled Person*, 1919

O littlest cloud in all the blue,
Don't go so fast, for, see,
I'm just about the size of you!
Come down and play with me!

But oh, if that's the only way—
To come in raindrops, why,
I'll stay here by myself and play!
I wouldn't have you cry!

"When you change the way you look at things, the
things you look at change." – Wayne Dyer

## WINDY NIGHTS
Robert Louis Stevenson (1850-1894), published in
*A Child's Garden of Verses*, 1885

Whenever the moon and stars are set,
    Whenever the wind is high,
  All night long in the dark and wet,
    A man goes riding by.
Late in the night when the fires are out,
Why does he gallop and gallop about?

Whenever the trees are crying aloud,
    And ships are tossed at sea,
  By, on the highway, low and loud,
    By at the gallop goes he;
By at the gallop he goes, and then
By he comes back at the gallop again.

"The riddles of God are more satisfying than the
solutions of man." – G. K. Chesterton

## THE JOURNEY
Eleanor Smith, published in
*American Primary Teacher: Volume 26*, 1902

Some little drops of water,
  Whose home was in a sea,
To go upon a journey
  Once happened to agree.
A cloud they had for carriage,
  Their horse a playful breeze,
And over land and country
  They rode awhile at ease.

But ah! There were so many,
  At last the carriage broke,
And to the ground came tumbling
  These frightened little folk.
And through the moss and grasses
  They were compelled to roam,
Until a brooklet found them
  And carried them all home.

"When you put your hand in a flowing stream, you touch the last that has gone before and the first that is still to come." – Leonardo da Vinci

## Waiting to Grow
Frank French, published in
*Songs of the Tree-top and Meadow*, 1899

Little white snowdrop just waking up,
Violet, daisy, and sweet buttercup!
Think of the flowers that are under the snow,
  Waiting to grow!

And think what hosts of queer little seeds—
Of flowers and mosses, of ferns and of weeds—
Are under the leaves, and under the snow,
  Waiting to grow!

Think of the roots getting ready to sprout,
Reaching their slender brown fingers about,
Under the ice, and the leaves, and the snow,
  Waiting to grow!

No seed is so small, or hidden so well,
That God cannot find it, and very soon tell
His sun where to shine, and His rain where to go,
  To help them to grow!

"Adopt the pace of Nature: her secret is patience."
Ralph Waldo Emerson

## THE COMING OF SPRING
E. M. P., published in *American Primary Teacher: Volume 32*, 1908

The birds are coming home soon;
　　I look for them every day;
I listen to catch the first wild strain
　　For they must be singing by May.

The bluebird, he'll come first you know,
　　Like a violet that has taken wings;
And the red-breast trills while his nest he builds,
　　I can hum the song that he sings.

And the crocus and wind-flower are coming, too;
　　They're already upon the way;
When the sun warms the brown earth through and
　　through,
　　I shall look for them *any* day.

Then be patient, and wait a little, my dear;
　　"They're coming," the winds repeat;
"We're coming!" We're coming!" I'm sure I hear,
　　From the grass blades that grow at my feet.

"For see, the winter is past,
the rains are over and gone.
The flowers appear on the earth,
the time of pruning the vines has come,
and the song of the turtledove is heard in our land."
Song of Songs 2:11-12

## FOG
Carl Sandburg (1878-1967), published in
*Chicago Poems*, 1918

The fog comes
on little cat feet.

It sits looking
over harbor and city
on silent haunches
and then moves on.

## THE FOG
Nancy Minerva (Haynes) Miller (1831-????), published
in *Mother Truth's Melodies*, 1879

"What is the fog, mamma?"

"Sometimes the air is light,
And cannot bear up all the mists,
And then 'tis foggy, quite.

"But, when air heavier grows,
The fog is borne above,
And floated off, the cloudy stuff,
Just see it, graceful, move."

"You can walk in a dream while you are awake: Just
walk in the misty morning of a forest!"
Mehmet Murat ildan

## Tardy Spring

George Meredith (1828–1909), published in
*The Works of George Meredith*, 1910

Now the North wind ceases,

The warm South-west awakes;
Swift fly the fleeces,
Thick the blossom-flakes. . . .

But now the North wind ceases,
The warm South-west awakes,
The heavens are out in fleeces,
And earth's green banner shakes.

"'Is the spring coming?' he said. 'What is it like?'" . . .
'It is the sun shining on the rain and the rain falling on
the sunshine, and things pushing up and working
under the earth.'" – Frances Hodgson Burnett,
*The Secret Garden*

## THE WOODPECKER
Elizabeth Madox Roberts (1881-1941),
published in *Under the Tree*, 1922

The woodpecker pecked out a little round hole
And made him a house in the telephone pole.

One day when I watched he poked out his head,
And he had on a hood and a collar of red.

When the streams of rain pour out of the sky,
And the sparkles of lightning go flashing by,

And the big, big wheels of thunder roll,
He can snuggle back in the telephone pole.


## THE WOODPECKER
Abbie Farwell Brown (1871-1927),
published in *Songs of Sixpence*, 1914

The woodpecker is such a bore!
   He's always knocking at the door
Of some old tree with horrid din,
   To see if any one is in.

He's never welcome where he goes,
   Because he's greedy, I suppose.
The trees all sigh beneath their breath:
   "Oh, dear! He bores us 'most to death!"


"Lo, these are but the outlines of his ways,
and what a whisper of a word we hear of him:
Who can comprehend the thunder of his power?"
Job 26:14

## PUSSY WILLOW

Ella Gardiner, published in
"St. Nicholas: Volume 10, 1883

Oh, you pussy willow,
Pretty little thing,
Coming with the sunshine
Of the merry spring;
Oh, tell me, tell me, pussy,
For I want to know,
Where is it you come from?
How is it you grow?

Now, my little children,
If you look at me,
And my little sisters
I am sure you'll see
Tiny little houses
Out of which we peep,
When we first are waking
From our winter's sleep.

As the days grow milder,
Out we put our heads,
And we lightly move us
In our little beds;
And when warmer breezes
Of the springtime blow,
Then we little pussies,
All to catkins grow.

"Let nature be your teacher." – William Wordsworth

## WHO LIKES THE RAIN?

Clara Doty Bates (1838-1895), published in
*Weather Opinions*, 1907

**"I"**, said the duck, "I call it fun,
For I have my little red rubbers on;
They make a cunning three-toed track
In the soft, cool mud. Quack! Quack! Quack!"

"I," cried the dandelion, "I,
My roots are thirsty, my buds are dry;"
And she lifted a tousled yellow head
Out of her green and grassy bed.

"I hope 'twill pour! I hope 'twill pour!"
Purred the tree toad at his gray back door,
"For, with a broad leaf for a roof,
I am perfectly weatherproof."

Sang the brook: "I laugh at every drop,
And wish they never need to stop
Till a big, big river I grew to be,
And could find my way out to the sea."

"I am in love with this green earth; the face of town
and country; the unspeakable rural solitudes. . . "
Charles Lamb

## ST. PATRICK'S BREASTPLATE
### St. Patrick (389?-461)

I bind unto myself today

The power of God to hold and lead,
His eye to watch, His might to stay,
His ear to hearken to my need:
The wisdom of my God to teach,
His hand to guide, His shield to ward;
The Word of God to give me speech,
His heavenly host to be my guard

Christ be with me,
Christ within me,
Christ behind me,
Christ before me,
Christ beside me,
Christ to win me,
Christ to comfort me and restore me,
Christ beneath me,
Christ above me,
Christ in the hearts of all that love me,
Christ in the mouth of friend and stranger.

"For Christians, believing in one God who is trinitarian communion suggests that the Trinity has left its mark on all creation. Saint Bonaventure went so far as to say that human beings, before sin, were able to see how each creature 'testifies that God is three.' . . . The Franciscan saint teaches us that *each creature bears in itself a specifically Trinitarian structure.* . . "
Laudato Si' 239

## AWAKENING

Margaret Sangster (1838-1912), published in
*Easter Bells: Poems*, 1897

Never yet was a springtime,
    Late though lingered the snow,
That the sap stirred not at the whisper
    Of the south wind, sweet and low;
Never yet was a springtime
    When the buds forgot to blow.

Ever the wings of the summer
    Are folded under the mold;
Life that has known no dying
    Is Love's to have and to hold,
Till sudden, the burgeoning Easter!
    The song! The green and the gold!

"Nature does not hurry, yet everything is
accomplished." – Lao Tzu

## GREAT SAINT JOSEPH, SON OF DAVID

Published in *The St. Gregory Hymnal and Catholic Choir Book*, 1920

Great Saint Joseph! Son of David,
Foster father of our Lord,
Spouse of Mary ever Virgin,
Keeping o'er them watch and ward!
In the stable you did guard them
With a father's loving care;
You by God's command did save them
From the cruel Herod's snare.

Three long days in grief and anguish
With His Mother sweet and mild,
Mary Virgin, did you wander
Seeking the beloved Child.
In the temple you did find Him:
Oh! What joy then filled your heart!
In your sorrows, in your gladness
Grant us, Joseph, to have a part.

Clasped in Jesus' arms and Mary's,
When death gently came at last,
Your pure spirit sweetly sighing
From its earthly dwelling passed.
Dear Saint Joseph! By that passing
May our death be like to thine;
And with Jesus, Mary, Joseph,
May our souls forever shine.

"Joseph rose and took the child and his mother by night and departed for Egypt. He stayed there until the death of Herod . . ." – Matthew 2:14-15

## OUT OF DOORS ARITHMETIC
F. M. L., published in *Primary Education:*
*Volume 3*, 1894

Add bright buds, and sun, and flowers,
New green leaves and fitful showers;
To a bare world, and the sum
Of the whole to "Spring" will come.

Multiply these leaves by more
And the flowers by a score;
The result—if found aright—
Will be "Summer" long and bright.

Then divide the flowers and sun
By gray clouds and storms begun,
And the quotient found will be
"Autumn" over land and sea.

From this then subtract the red
Of the leaves up overhead—
Also every flower in sight,
And you've "Winter" cold and white

"Ere man is aware that spring is here, the flowers have
found it out." – Chinese Proverb

## MARCH

Celia Thaxter (1835-1894), published in
*Poems for Children*, 1884

I wonder what spendthrift chose to spill
Such bright gold under my window-sill!
Is it fairy gold? Does it glitter still?
Bless me! It is but a daffodil!

And look at the crocuses, keeping tryst*
With the daffodil by the sunshine kissed!
Like beautiful baubles of amethyst
They seem, blown out of the earth's snow-mist. . . .
Who said that March was a scold and a shrew?

Who said she had nothing on earth to do
But tempests and furies and rages to brew?
Why, look at the wealth she has lavished on you!

O March that blusters, and March that blows,
What color under your footstep glows?
Beauty you summon from winter's snows
And you are the pathway that leads to the rose.

* a private meeting

"I, the invisible,
March, the earth-shaker,
March, the sea-lifter,
March, the sky-render."
Isabella Valancy Crawford

## THE CATKIN

Kate Louise Brown (1837-1921), published in
*The Plant Baby and Its Friends*, 1897

Pretty little catkin,
Swinging in the sun;
Pretty little catkin,
Has your work begun?

You are stretching downward;
Do you want to see
Just how long a catkin,
Growing well, may be?

Pretty little catkin,
Now your blossoms part,
And the yellow pollen
Scatters from your heart,

Other seeds to ripen:
This is what you do.
Growing time is pleasant
Both for us and you.

Pretty little catkin,
Swinging in the sun;
Pretty little catkin,
Then your work is done.

"Anyone who keeps the ability to see beauty never
grows old." – Franz Kafka

## THE BROOK
James Whitcomb Riley (1849-1916), published in
*Joyful Poems for Children*, 1892

Little brook! Little brook!
You have such a happy look—
Such a very merry manner, as you swerve and
curve and crook—
And your ripples, one and one,
Reach each other's hands and run
Like laughing little children in the sun!

## I LIKE THE BROOK
Annette Wynne (died 1953), published in
*For Days and Days*, 1919

I like the brook, I like the tree,
The solemn-sounding rolling sea,
The little roads where children stray—
I like to like things all the day.

"Everybody should be quiet near a little stream
and listen." – Ruth Krauss

## LITTLE BY LITTLE
Published in "Arthur's Home Magazine:
Volume IX", 1857

"Little by little," an acorn said,
As it slowly sank in its mossy bed;
"I am improving every day,
Hidden deep in the earth away."

Little by little it sipped the dew,
Little by little each day it grew;
Downward it sent out a threadlike root,
Up in the air sprang a tiny shoot.

Day after day and year after year,
Little by little the leaves appear;
And the slender branches spread far and wide,
Till the mighty oak is the forest's pride.

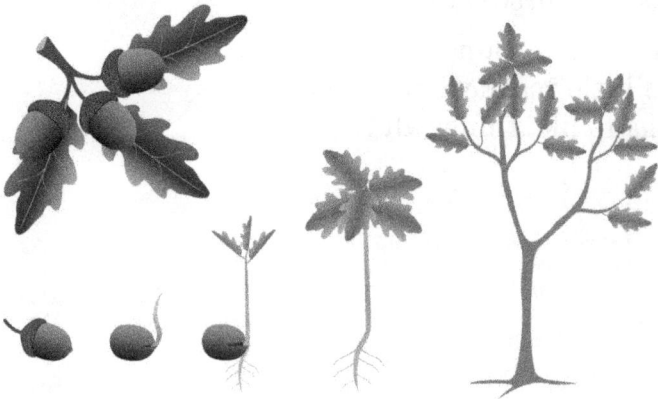

"The creation of a thousand forests is in one acorn."
Ralph Waldo Emerson

## HAIL! FULL OF GRACE

Sister Mary Josita Belger (1899-1978), published in
*Sing a Song of Holy Things*, 1945

An angel came to Mary's home
  Many years ago.
Our lovely lady knelt in prayer,
  With head bowed down, when lo!

"Hail, Full of grace!" The angel said,
  "Oh, Mary, blest art thou!"
She gathered close her mantle blue,
  And with a holy bow,

In prayer and fear she heard the word
  Sent by the Father's love.
She would be Mother of His Son,
  The Son of God above.

The Holy Virgin once again
  Bowed low her queenly head,
"Behold the handmaid of the Lord!
  Be it done to me," she said.

The angel carried back the word
  To God the Father then,
The word that meant that heaven's gates
  Would open now to men.

"Then the angel said to her, 'Do not be afraid, Mary,
for you have found favor with God. Behold, you will
conceive in your womb and bear a son, and you
shall name him Jesus.'" – Luke 1:30-31

## GRASS BLADES
Published in *Popular Educator:*
*Volume 13,* 1895

Peeping, peeping, here and there

In lawns and meadows everywhere
Coming up to find the Spring
And hear the robin-redbreast sing.
Creeping under children's feet,
Glancing at the violets sweet,
Growing into tiny bowers,
For the dainty meadow flowers—
We are small, but think a minute
Of a world with no grass in it.

"God, I can push the grass apart
And lay my finger on Thy heart!"
Edna St. Vincent Millay, "Renascence"

## THE LITTLE PLANT
Kate Louise Brown (1837-1921), published in
*The Plant Baby and Its Friends*, 1897

In the heart of a seed
Buried deep, so deep,
A dear little plant
Lay fast asleep.

"Wake!" said the sunshine
"And creep to the light,"
"Wake!" said the voice
Of the raindrops bright.

The little plant heard,
And it rose to see
What the wonderful
Outside world might be.

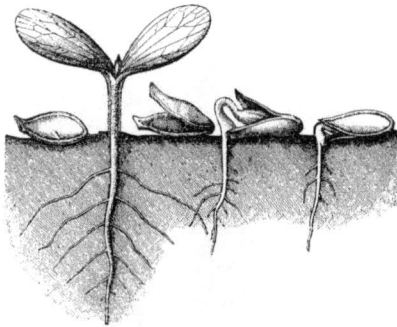

"Always be on the lookout for the presence of
wonder." – E. B. White

# St. Xystus (Pope St. Sixtus III)

Robert Hugh Benson (1871-1914), published in
*An Alphabet of Saints*, 1906

## "X"
for ST. XYSTUS, a very old man,

Who was Pope when a great persecution began.
He had a young Deacon, St. LAWRENCE, and they
Were both carried off to the Judges one day;
Some cowards to idols and sprites sacrificed,
But XYSTUS and LAWRENCE were faithful to
    CHRIST,
For though they were tortured they wouldn't give in,
But chose rather to die than commit such a sin;
And so they were able their courage to keep,
And like the GOOD SHEPHERD both died for the
    Sheep.

(ST. XYSTUS or ST. SIXTUS III, Pope and Martyr,
Pope from September, 255, to his Martyrdom in 258.
Feast March 28)

"'For whoever wishes to save his life will lose it, but
whoever loses his life for my sake will save it. What
profit is there for one to gain the whole world yet lose
or forfeit himself?'" – Luke 9:24-25

## A SPRING SONG
Published in *A Jolly Jingle-Book*, 1913

Out in the woods,
Where the wild birds sing,
It is all alive
With the happy spring.

It gets in my feet,
And the first I know
They are dancing-glad,
And away they go.

I race with the brook
Till my breath is gone,
And it laughs at me
As it races on.

I rock with the trees,
And I sway and swing,
And make believe
I am part of the spring.

"Going to the woods is going home." – John Muir

## MIRACLE
L. H. Bailey, published in
*The Melody of Earth*, 1918

Yesterday the twig was brown and bare;

Today the glint of green is there.
Tomorrow will be leaflets spare;
I know no thing so wondrous fair,
No miracle so strangely rare.
I wonder what will next be there!

## CERTAINTY
Emily Dickinson (1830-1886), published in
*Poems of the English Race*, 1921

I never saw a moor,

I never saw the sea;
Yet know I how the heather looks,
And what a wave must be.

I never spoke with God,
Nor visited in heaven;
Yet certain am I of the spot
As if the chart were given.

"The most astonishing thing about miracles is that
they happen." – G. K. Chesterton

March 31

## THE DAY BEFORE APRIL

Mary Carolyn Davies (1888-1940?), published in
*Youth Riding* (1919)

The day before April

Alone, alone,
I walked in the wood
And sat on a stone.

I sat on a broad stone
And sang to the birds.
The tune was God's making
But I made the words.

## THE DAY BEFORE APRIL

Mary Carolyn Davies (1888-1940?), published in
*A Little Freckled Person*, 1919

No, little brown bird, go away,

I have no time to dream today.
I must do certain things, you see.
I know not why, but it must be!
Here I must study foolish books,
And not guess how the lilac looks!

Hush, little bird, and do not sing!
I have no time to play with Spring!

"The trees and the stones will teach you what you will
never learn from the masters."
St. Bernard of Clairvaux

# APRIL

## AN APRIL DAY

Rachel G. Smith, published in
*Child's Calendar Beautiful*, 1905

Take a dozen little clouds
And a little patch of blue;
Take a million raindrops
As many sunbeams too.

Take a host of violets,
A wandering little breeze,
And myriads of little leaves
Dancing on the trees.

Then mix them well together,
In the very quickest way,
Showers and sunshine, birds and flowers,
And you'll have an April day.

> "EVER SINCE THE CREATION OF THE WORLD, HIS INVISIBLE ATTRIBUTES OF ETERNAL POWER AND DIVINITY HAVE BEEN ABLE TO BE UNDERSTOOD AND PERCEIVED IN WHAT HE HAS MADE. . . ." – ROMANS 1:20

## APRIL FOOLS' DAY
Published in *Poor Robin's Almanack*, 1790

The first of April, some do say

Is set apart for All Fool's Day;
But why the people call it so
Nor I, nor they themselves, do know.
But on this day are people sent
On purpose for pure merriment.

"Foolish by nature were all who were in ignorance of
God, and who from the good things seen did not
succeed in knowing the one who is, and from
studying the works did not discern the artisan;"
Wisdom 13:1

## THE FIRST BLUEBIRD

James Whitcomb Riley (1849-1916), published in
*The Complete Works of James Whitcomb Riley:
Volume I*, 1913

Jest rain and snow! and rain again!
  And dribble! drip! and blow!
Then snow! and thaw! and slush! and then—
  Some more rain and snow!

This morning I was 'most afeard
  To wake up—when, I jing!
I seen the sun shine out and heerd
  The first blue-bird of Spring!—
Mother she'd raised the winder some;—
And in acrost the orchard come,
  Soft as an angel's wing,
A breezy, treesy, beesy hum,
  Too sweet for anything!

The winter's shroud was rent apart—
  The sun bust forth in glee,—
And when that blue-bird sung, my hart
  Hopped out o' bed with me!

"Sweet spring, full of sweet days and roses;
A box where sweets compacted lie."
George Herbert

## APRIL

Sara Teasdale (1884-1933), published in
*Rivers to the Sea,* 1915

The roofs are shining from the rain,

The sparrows twitter as they fly,
And with a windy April grace
The little clouds go by.

Yet the back yards are bare and brown
With only one unchanging tree—
I could not be so sure of spring
Save that it sings in me.

"Well apparell'd April on the heel of limping winter
treads." – William Shakespeare.

## THE RAIN
Published in *Songs of the Tree-top and Meadow*, 1899

Down falls the pleasant rain
To water thirsty flowers;
Then shines the sun again,
To cheer this earth of ours.

If it were always rain
The flowers would be drowned.
If it were always sun,
No flowers would be found.


## MUD
Polly Chase Boyden, published in *Toward Equilibrium*, 1930

Mud is very nice to feel
All squishy-squash between the toes!
I'd rather wade in wiggly mud
Than smell a yellow rose.

Nobody else but the rosebush knows
How nice mud feels
Between the toes.


"In the spring, at the end of the day, you should smell like dirt." – Margaret Atwood

## APRIL'S WIND
Daniel A. Lord (1888-1955), published in
*Chants for Children*, 1942

When April comes, our kites we fly
Away, way up into the sky.
Someday we'll fly our airplanes there,
And larks and eagles best beware.

The April wind that lifts our kite
Lifts flowers and shrubs for our delight,
And at its shouting, flowers are born
To stand on guard for Easter morn.

For April wind blew fierce and loud
And angry o'er the Calvary crowd.
New every year its trumpet blows
To say, "This morning Christ arose."

Ah, wind of April, magic breeze,
That frees the flowers and clothes the trees,
Blow as you will, in each direction
Tell all the earth of Resurrection.

". . . Stand and consider the marvels of God!"
Job 37:14

## IN APRIL

Emily Huntington Miller (1833-1913), published in
*From Avalon and Other Poems*, 1896

April! That's the time o' year
When the earth is waking;
When with every morn you see
Signs there's no mistaking.

When the wind is blowing south,
And the rain's soft pelting
Sets the little brooks a-brim
And the last snow melting;

When the grass begins to show
Greener in the hollows;
When the robin calls his mate
And the bluebird follows;

When the wild geese scream at night,
To the northward hasting;
When the maple bark is wet
With the sweet sap wasting—

April! That's the time o' year
Life and love are stirring;
Throb of heart, and leap of blood,
Rush of soft wings whirring!

"Once more the ancient Wonder
Brings back the goose and crane,
Prophetic Sons of Thunder,
Apostles of the Rain. . . ."
John G. Neibardt, "Easter—1923"

## HOW THE FLOWERS GROW

Margaret Eytinge (1832-1916), published in "St. Nicholas: Volume 2, Part 1", 1875

First a seed so tiny
Hidden from the sight,
Then two pretty leaflets
Struggling toward the light;
Soon a bud appearing
Turns into a flower,
Kissed by golden sunshine,
Washed by silver shower;
Growing sweeter, sweeter,
Every happy hour!
Kissed by golden sunshine,
Washed by silver shower.

"The earth laughs in flowers." – Ralph Waldo Emerson

## APRIL! APRIL! ARE YOU HERE?
Dora Read Goodale (1866-1953), published in
*Primary Education: Volume 5,* 1897

April! April! Are you here?
Oh, how fresh the wind is blowing!
See! The sky is bright and clear,
Oh, how green the grass is growing!
April! April! Are you here?

April! April! Is it you?
See how fair the flowers are springing!
Sun is warm and brooks are clear,
Oh, how glad the birds are singing!
April! April! Is it you?

April! April! You are here!
Though your smiling turn to weeping,
Though your skies grow cold and drear,
Though your gentle winds are sleeping,
April! April! You are here!

"All nature seems so full of God to me, the wind
blowing in the tall trees, the little birds singing, the
beautiful blue sky, everything speaks to me of Him."
St. Elizabeth of the Trinity, *He Is My Heaven*

## BUDS

Mary Carolyn Davies (1888-1940?), published in
*A Little Freckled Person*, 1919

The buds have come to town;
Demure and brown
Their coats; and under, see,
How can such fragile, fairy colors be?

The buds have come to us
All tremulous.
We're quite as glad as they.
Take off your cloaks, dear little buds, and stay!

## NEW LEAVES

Mary Carolyn Davies (1888-1940?), published in *A Little Freckled Person*, 1919

It doesn't do you any good to hide,

Trees! Everybody knows you're there inside!
Besides, although you think you're hid complete
—We see your feet!

"Blessed are they who see beautiful things in humble
places where other people see nothing."
Camille Pissarro

## To the First Robin

Lousia May Alcott (1832-1888), written in 1840, published in *Louisa May Alcott: Her Life, Letters, and Journals*, 1889

"Welcome, welcome, little stranger,
Fear no harm, and fear no danger;
We are glad to see you here,
For you sing 'Sweet Spring is near.'"

Now the white snow melts away;
Now the flowers blossom gay.
Come dear bird and build your nest,
For we love our robin best.

"Nothing in the world is quite as adorably lovely as a robin when he shows off—and they are nearly always doing it." – Frances Hodgson Burnett

## THE BLUEBIRD (FROM)
Eben Eugene Rexford (1848-1916), published in
*The Spring Months*, 1907

Never the song of the robin

Could make my heart so glad;
When I hear the bluebird singing
In spring, I forget to be sad.
Hear it! A ripple of music!
Sunshine changed into song!
It sets me thinking of summer
When the days and their dreams are long.

## THE BLUEBIRD
Rev. John B. Tabb (1845-1909), published in
*Child Verse*, 1900

When God had made a host of them,

One little flower still lacked a stem
To hold its blossom blue;
So into it He breathed a song,
And suddenly, with petals strong
As wings, away it flew.

"I used to believe that prayer changes things, but now I know that prayer changes us and we change things." – St. Teresa of Calcutta

## Hepatica

Anna M. Pratt, published in *All the Year Round*, 1896

When April awakens the blossom folk,
 And bluebirds are on the wing,
Hepatica muffled in downy cloak,
 Hastens to greet the spring.

Careless of cold when northwind blows,
 Glad when the sun shines down,
She opens her wrap, and smiling, shows
 Her dainty lavender gown.

Her sisters are robed in pink, and some
 Are in royal purple dressed,
And over the hills and fields they come
 To welcome the darling guest.

The children laugh as they pick the flowers,
 And the happy robins sing;
For, blooming in chill and leafless bowers,
 Hepatica means the spring.

"The world will never starve for want of wonders, but
only for want of wonder." – C. S. Lewis

## CROCUS
Kate Louise Brown (1837-1921), published in
*The Plant Baby and Its Friends*, 1897

'T was a little aimless snowflake
That the jeering north wind blew,
Very lonely, quite discouraged,
Undecided what to do.

So it fell beneath my window,
On our Mother Earth's brown breast;
Glad to think its journey over,
Happy in its thought of rest.

From the gray cloud's sullen border
Crept a little beam of gold;
Just a patch of blue sky shimmered
As it kissed the frozen mold.

Did the blue sky and the sunbeam
Weave a spell of magic power?
In the morning, 'neath my window,
Smiled a fairy crocus flower!

"Above all, watch with glittering eyes the whole world
around you because the greatest secrets are always
hidden in the most unlikely places. Those who don't
believe in magic will never find it." – Roald Dahl

## THE TREE OUTSIDE
Annette Wynne (died 1953), published in
*For Days and Days*, 1919

The tree outside stands straight and tall
And never can lie down at all;
For if it once should take a rest,
I fear for each small swinging nest;
And so untiredly it stands
And holds up in its leafy hands
The little nests; and soon and late
I bless my good tree, tall and straight,
I bless its kind strong loving arms,
That hold the birds and nests from harms,
It never does grow tired at all,
I love you, Tree, straight, kind, and tall.

"A taste for the beautiful is most cultivated out of
doors, where there is no house and no housekeeper."
Henry David Thoreau

## DAFFODILS
William Wordsworth (1770-1850)
Written April 15, 1802

I wandered lonely as a cloud
That floats on high o'er vales and hills,
When all at once I saw a crowd,
A host, of golden daffodils;
Beside the lake, beneath the trees,
Fluttering and dancing in the breeze.

Continuous as the stars that shine
And twinkle on the Milky Way,
They stretched in never-ending line
Along the margin of a bay;
Ten thousand saw I at a glance,
Tossing their heads in sprightly dance. . . .

The waves beside them danced; but they
Outdid the sparkling waves in glee;
A poet could not but be gay
In such a jocund* company;
I gazed—and gazed—but little thought
What wealth the show to me had brought.

For oft, when on my couch I lie
In vacant or in pensive mood,
They flash upon that inward eye
Which is the bliss of solitude;
And then my heart with pleasure fills,
And dances with the daffodils.


* happy; joyful


"The man is richest whose pleasures are the cheapest." – Henry David Thoreau

## THE BLUEBIRD'S SONG TO THE FLOWERS
Emily Huntington Miller (1833-1913), published in
*An Outline for Plant Study*, 1897

I know the song that the bluebird is singing,

Out in the apple tree where he is swinging.
Brave little fellow! The skies may be dreary—
Nothing cares he while his heart is so cheery.

Hark! How the music leaps out from his throat!
Hark! Was there ever so merry a note?
Listen a while, and you'll hear what he's saying,
Up in the apple tree swinging and swaying.

"Dear little blossoms down under the snow,
You must be weary of winter I know.
Listen, I'll sing you a message of cheer!
Summer is coming! And springtime is here!

"Little white snowdrop! I pray you arise;
Bright yellow crocus! Please open your eyes;
Sweet little violets, hid from the cold,
Put on your mantles of purple and gold;
Daffodils! Daffodils! Say, do you hear?—
Summer is coming, and springtime is here!"

"Maternal old apple trees, regular old grandmothers,
who have seen trouble." – John Burroughs

## THE ROBIN
### Traditional English Song, published in
*Murby's Imperial*, 1879

There came to my window, one morning in spring,

A sweet little robin, he came there to sing;
The tune he was singing was prettier far
Than any I heard on the flute or guitar.
He raised his light wings to fly off away,
But resting a moment seemed sweetly to say,
"How happy, how happy the world seems to be;
Awake, little child, and be happy with me."

## EARLY BIRD
### Daniel A. Lord (1888-1955), published in
*Chants for Children*, 1942

However early I may be,

The robin's up ahead of me,
His breakfast eaten, prayers all said,
And calling me a sleepy head.
But someday soon, I give my word,
I'm going to beat that early bird.

"I have never heard anything sweeter than the
whistling of the robins at sunset in the maple woods . . ."
L. M. Montgomery

## APRIL (FROM)
Edwin (Ted) Meade Robinson (1878-1946), published in
*Mere Melodies*, 1918

So here we are in April, in showy, blowy April,

In frowsy, blowsy April, the rowdy dowdy time
In soppy, sloppy April, in wheezy breezy April,
In ringing, stinging April, with a singing swinging
    rhyme. . . .
So here we are in April, in tipsy gypsy April,
In showery, flowery April, the twinkly, sprinkly
    days;
In tingly, jingly April, in highly wily April,
In mighty, flighty April with its highty-tighty ways!

". . . Proud-pied April, dress'd in all his trim,
Hath put a spirit of youth in everything."
William Shakespeare

## HOW THE VIOLETS CAME
Published in *Songs of the Tree-top and Meadow*, 1899

I know—blue, modest violets,
  Gleaming with the dew of morn,
I know the place you came from
  And the way that you were born.
When God cut holes in Heaven—
  The holes the stars look through—
He let the scraps fall down to earth:
  The little scraps are you.


## THE BIRTH OF THE FLOWERS
Mary McNeil Fenollosa, published in
*The Melody of Earth*, 1918

God spoke! And from the arid scene

Sprang rich and verdant bowers,
Till all the earth was soft with green,—
He smiled; and there were flowers.


"God is the perfect poet." – Robert Browning

## VIOLETS
Christina Rossetti (1830-1894), published in
*Sing Song, A Nursery Rhyme Book*, 1872

O wind, where have you been,

That you blow so sweet?
Among the violets
Which blossom at your feet.

The honeysuckle waits
For summer and for heat.
But violets in the chilly spring
Make the turf so sweet.

## GOD
Rev. John B. Tabb (1845-1909), published in
*The Violet Book,* 1909

I see Thee in the distant blue

But in the violet's dell of dew,
Behold, I *breathe* and *touch* Thee, too.

"And so it is in the world of souls, Jesus' garden. He
willed to create great souls comparable to Lilies and
roses, but He has created smaller ones and these
must be content to be daisies or violets destined to
give joy to God's glances when He looks down at His
feet. Perfection consists in doing His will, in being what
He wills us to be." – St. Therese of Lisieux

## APRIL SHOWERS
Mary E. Wilkins (1852-1930), published in
*Child's Own Speaker*, 1915

There fell an April shower one night:
Next morning, in the garden-bed,
The crocuses stood straight and gold:
"And they have come," the children said.

There fell an April shower one night:
Next morning, thro' the woodland spread
The Mayflowers, pink and sweet as youth:
"And they are come," the children said.

There fell an April shower one night:
Next morning, sweetly, overhead,
The blue-birds sung, the blue-birds sung:
"And they have come," the children said.

"If you have a garden and a library, you have
everything you need." – Marcus Tullius Cicero

## GOD'S OUTDOORS

Sr. M. Paraclita McTigue (1889-1984), published in
*American Cardinal Reader, Volume Two*, 1929

The grass is a beautiful carpet,

And a vast, blue roof is the sky;
The trees are like huge umbrellas,
When the sun is hot and high.

The snow is a soft, white blanket,
Laid on when the days are cold;
And the ice is a clear, bright mirror,
That winter likes to hold.

To enjoy and love all seasons
We are not too young or small;
How good is our dear Creator,
The Lord and Maker of all!

"We do not inherit the earth from our ancestors;
we borrow it from our children."
Wendell Berry/Moses Henry Cass

## EARLY NEWS
Anna M. Pratt, published in *An American Anthology:*
*1787-1899,* 1900

The sparrow told it to the robin,

The robin told it to the wren,
Who passed it on with sweet remark
To thrush and bobolink and lark,
The news,
That dawn had come again.

## THE MORNING LARK
Annette Wynne (died 1953), published in
*Treasure Things,* 1922

The morning lark rose early

To see the black dark go,
"Goodbye, dear Dark," sang the morning Lark,
"Good morning, Morning-Glow!"

"The world is always young again for just a few
moments at the dawn." – Emily in *Emily Climbs*
by L. M. Montgomery

## THE BIRD'S PRAYER
Published in *The Ideal Catholic Reader,
Second Reader*, 1915

"Pretty little song bird,

Happy as a king,
Will you tell me truly
Why is it you sing?"

"Early in the morning.
At the break of day,
High up in the blue sky.
In sweet tones I pray.

"I praise God the Father
Every time I sing;
I then pay my homage
To the Great High King."

## CHORUS OF BIRDS
### (FROM "THE MASQUE OF PANDORA")

Henry Wadsworth Longfellow (1807-1882), published in
*The Masque of Pandora and Other Poems*, 1876

Every flutter of the wing,

Every note of song we sing,
Every murmur, every tone,
Is of love and love alone.

"I hear the chorus, it is a grand opera,
Ah, this indeed is music—this suits me."
Walt Whitman, "Song of Myself"

## WHAT ROBIN TOLD

George Cooper (1840-1927), published in
*Songs of the Tree-top and Meadow*, 1899

How do robins build their nests?
   Robin Redbreast told me.
First a wisp of yellow hay
In a pretty round they lay;
Then some shreds of downy floss,
Feather, too, and bits of moss,
Woven with a sweet, sweet song,
This way, that way, and across;
   That's what robin told me.

Where do robins hide their nests?
   Robin Redbreast told me.
Up among the leaves so deep,
Where the sunbeams rarely creep;
Long before the winds are cold,
Long before the leaves are gold,
Bright-eyed stars will peep and see
Baby robins—one, two, three;
   That's what robin told me.

"Robins and wrens,
Are God's good friends."
English Rhyme

## THE SECRET
Darthea E. Eno (age 8), published in "St Nicholas:
Volume 36, Part 2," 1909

We have a secret, just we three,
The robin, and I, and the sweet cherry tree;
The bird told the tree and the tree told me,
And nobody knows it but just we three.

But of course the robin knows it best,
Because he built the—I shan't tell the rest,
And laid the four little—something's in it—
I'm afraid I shall tell it every minute.

But if the tree and the robin don't peep,
I'll try my best the secret to keep;
Though I know when the little birds fly about,
Then the whole secret will be out.

"Each thing in nature holds a secret and its existence
is the unfolding of this secret under the watchful,
loving attention of God." – Wayne Simsic,
*Natural Prayer*

# St. Zita

Robert Hugh Benson (1871-1914), published in
*An Alphabet of Saints*, 1906

**"Z"** for ST. ZITA, the good kitchen-maid;

She prayed, and she prayed, and she prayed, and
    she prayed;
One morning she got so absorbed in her prayers,
She simply neglected her household affairs.
Too late she remembered 'twas bread-making day,
And she trembled to think what her mistress
    would say.
She flew to the oven, looked in it, and cried,
"Glory be to the LORD! the bread's ready inside!"
The Angels had kneaded it, raised it with yeast,
Made the fire, put the pans in the oven—at least
I can only suppose that was how it was done,
For the bread was all baked by a quarter to one.
    To pray like St. ZITA, but not to be late,
    Is the way to be good, and (if possible) great.

(ST. ZITA, Virgin; Born about 1210; Lived for forty-eight
years in the service of one Fatinelli, citizen of Lucca,
Italy; Died, 1272. Feast, April 27)

"Be who you were meant to be, and you will set the
world on fire." – St. Catherine of Siena

## APPLE BLOSSOM

Kate Brown (1837-1921), published in *Songs of the Tree-top and Meadow*, 1899

Lady Apple Blossom,
Just arrived in town,
Wears a light green bonnet
And a snowy gown.
The pretty dress is—
What do you think?
Five white petals
Just touched with pink.

## DAFFADOWNDILLY

Christina Rossetti (1830-1894), published in
*Sing Song, A Nursery Rhyme Book*, 1872

Growing in the vale
By the uplands hilly,
Growing straight and frail,
Lady Daffadowndilly.

In a golden crown,
And a scant green gown
While the spring blows chilly,
Lady Daffadown,
Sweet Daffadowndilly.

"Beauty is nature's fact."
Emily Dickinson, "The Earth Has Many Keys"

## THE DANDELION
Florence Marsh, published in
*All the Year Round*, 1896

Bright little dandelion,
Downy, yellow face,
Peeping up among the grass
With such gentle grace;
Minding not the April wind
Blowing rude and cold;
Brave little dandelion
With a heart of gold.

Meek little dandelion
Changing into curls
At the magic touch of these
Merry boys and girls.
When they pinch your dainty throat,
Strip your dress of green,
On your soft and gentle face
Not a cloud is seen.

Poor little dandelion,
Now all gone to seed,
Scattered roughly by the wind
Like a common weed.
You have lived your little life
Smiling every day;
Who could do a better thing
In a better way?

"God has made everything appropriate to its time . . ."
Ecclesiastes 3:11

## WHILE APRIL RAIN WENT BY

Shaemas O'Sheel (1886-1954), published in
*The Light Feet of Goats*, 1915

Under a budding hedge I hid
While April rain went by,
But little drops came slipping through,
Fresh from a laughing sky:

A-many little scurrying drops,
Laughing the song they sing,
Soon found me where I sought to hide,
And pelted me with spring.

And I lay back and let them pelt,
And dreamt deliciously
Of lusty leaves and lady-blossoms
And baby-buds I'd see.

When April rain had laughed the land
Out of its wintry way,
And coaxed all growing things to greet
With gracious garb the May.

"The hooded clouds, like friars,
Tell their beads in drops of rain." – Henry Wadsworth
Longfellow, "Midnight Mass for the Dying Year"

# MAY

### THE MONTH OF MAY
Anna Burnham Bryant, published in
*In Playland*, 1911

It comes just after April,
And right before 'tis June;
And every bird that's singing
Has this same lovely tune:
"You needn't ask your mother
To let you go and play;
The very breezes whisper,
'You may! You may! You may!'

"There are no frosts to freeze you,
And no fierce winds to blow;
But winds that seem like kisses,
So soft and sweet and slow.
The lovely sun is shining
'Most every single day.
Of course you may go out, dears—
It is the *month* of 'May'!"

> "I WANT CREATION TO PENETRATE YOU WITH SO MUCH ADMIRATION THAT WHEREVER YOU GO, THE LEAST PLANT MAY BRING YOU CLEAR REMEMBRANCE OF THE CREATOR. A SINGLE PLANT, A BLADE OF GRASS, OR ONE SPECK OF DUST IS SUFFICIENT TO OCCUPY ALL YOUR INTELLIGENCE IN BEHOLDING THE ART WITH WHICH IT HAS BEEN MADE." – ST. BASIL

## JOY OF SAINT JOSEPH

Sister Mary Josita Belger (1899-1978), published in
*Sing a Song of Holy Things*, 1945

Saint Joseph was a busy man

And worked hard every day
To keep the Holy Family
From need along life's way.

He loved to see the Holy Child
Play near him on the floor
With bits of wood, and little nails,
And scraps of two-by-four.

Holy Joseph, happy man!
How great your daily joy
To work beside the God of love,
The Father's Baby Boy.

"A man who works with his hands is a laborer; a man who works with his hands and his brain is a craftsman; but a man who works with his hands and his brain and his heart is an artist."
Louis Nizer, *Between You and Me*

## MAY DAY

Sara Teasdale (1884-1933), published in
*Flame and Shadow*, 1920

A delicate fabric of bird song
　　Floats in the air,
The smell of wet wild earth
　　Is everywhere.

Red small leaves of the maple
　　Are clenched like a hand,
Like girls at their first communion
　　The pear trees stand.

Oh I must pass nothing by
　　Without loving it much,
The raindrop try with my lips,
　　The grass with my touch;

For how can I be sure
　　I shall see again
The world on the first of May
　　Shining after the rain?

"One touch of nature makes the whole world kin."
William Shakespeare

## THE QUEEN OF SEASONS
John Henry Newman (1801-1890), published in
*Selections of the Prose and Poems of John Henry
Newman*, 1907

. . . The freshness of May,
   and the sweetness of June,
And the fire of July
   in its passionate noon,
Munificent* August,
   September serene,
Are together no match
   for my glorious Queen.

O Mary, all months
   and all days are your own
In you lasts their joyousness,
   when they are gone;
And we give to you May,
   not because it is best,
But because it come first,
   and is pledge of the rest.

\* bountiful; generous

". . . he fixed the ordered seasons and the boundaries
of their regions, so that people might seek God . . ."
Acts 17:26-27

## EVENING SONG
Fannie Stearns Davis (1884-1966), published in
*Crack O' Dawn,* 1915

Little child, good child, go to sleep.

The tree-toads purr and the peepers peep.
Under the apple-tree grass grows deep;
Little child, good child, go to sleep!

Big star out in the orange west;
Orioles swung in their gypsy nest;
Soft wind singing what you love best;
Rest till the sunrise; rest, child, rest!

Swift dreams swarm in a silver flight—
Hand in hand with the sleepy Night.
Lie down soft with your eyelids tight.
Hush, child, little child! Hush.
—Good-night.—

"In peace I will lie down and fall asleep,
for you alone, LORD, make me secure." – Psalms 4:9

## WHO TAUGHT THE BIRD?
Jane Taylor (1783-1824), published in
*Mother-Song and Child Song*, 1898

Who taught the bird to build her nest
Of softest wool, and hay, and moss?
Who taught her how to weave it best,
 And lay the tiny twigs across?

Who taught the busy bee to fly
Among the sweetest herbs and flowers,
And lay her store of honey by,
Providing food for winter hours?

Who taught the little ant the way
Her narrow cell so well to bore
And through the pleasant summer day
To gather up her winter store?

'Twas God who taught them all the way,
And gave the little creatures skill;
He teaches children, when they pray,
To know and do His heavenly will.

"I believe that in each little thing created by God
there is more than is understood, even if it is a little
ant." – St. Teresa of Avila, *Interior Castle*

## MAY

George MacDonald (1824-1903), published in
*Song of the Tree-top and Meadow*, 1899

Merry, rollicking, frolicking May
Into the woods came skipping one day;
She teased the brook till he laughed outright,
And gurgled and scolded with all his might;
She chirped to the birds and bade them sing
A chorus of welcome to Lady Spring;
And the bees and butterflies she set
To waking the flowers that were sleeping yet.
She shook the trees till the buds looked out
To see what the trouble was all about,
And nothing in Nature escaped that day
The touch of life-giving, bright young May.

"How lovely is the silence of growing things."
Evan Dickens

## THE LEAFLETS
Kate Louise Brown (1837-1921), published in
*The Plant Baby and Its Friends*, 1897

Dance, little leaflets, dance,
'Neath the tender sky of spring!
Dance in the golden sun
To the tune the robins sing!
Now you are light and young,
Just fit for a baby play,
So dance, little leaflets, dance,
And welcome the merry May!

"In all things of nature, there is something of the
marvelous." - Aristotle

## AFTERNOON ON A HILL
Edna St. Vincent Millay (1892-1950), published in
*Renascence and Other Poems*, 1917

I will be the gladdest thing
Under the sun!
I will touch a hundred flowers
And not pick one.

I will look at cliffs and clouds
With quiet eyes,
Watch the wind bow down the grass,
And the grass rise.

And when lights begin to show
Up from the town,
I will mark which must be mine,
And then start down!

"When in the wilds, we must not carry our problems
with us or the joy is lost." – Sigurd Olson

## MAY

Ada Stewart Sheldon, published in
*Child's Calendar Beautiful,* 1905

O dear little maiden is dainty Miss May,
And she has such a pleasant and sweet winning
way,
That we long to be out and be with her all day.

She comes over the meadows and into the town
All embroidered with lilacs her beautiful gown,
And her bonnet of buttercups way to the crown.

When she smiles all the clouds disappear from
the skies,
For there's seldom a tear to be seen in those eyes,
Whose color to match the forget-me-not tries.

And to show how they love her, their own darling
May,
'Tis with blushes as pink as the dawn of the day,
That each apple tree turns to a blooming bouquet.

"I shall not go to town while the Lilacs bloom."
Henry Wadsworth Longfellow

## FATHER DAMIEN

Fr. John Bannister Tabb (1845-1909), published in
*A Selection from the Verses of John B. Tabb*, 1909

O God, the cleanest offering

Of tainted earth below,
Unblushing to Thy feet we bring—
*"A leper white as snow!"*

## FORGET-ME-NOT

Emily Bruce Roelofson (1832-??), published in
*Child's Calendar Beautiful*, 1906

W hen to the flowers so beautiful

The Father gave a name,
Back came a little blue-eyed one,—
All timidly it came.

And standing at the Father's feet
And gazing in His face,
It said, in meek and timid voice,
And with a modest grace:

"Dear Lord, the name You gave me,
Alas, I have forgot."
The Father kindly looked on her
And said, "Forget-me-not."

"Never lose an opportunity of seeing anything
beautiful, for beauty is God's handwriting."
Ralph Waldo Emerson

## SPRING

Celia Thaxter, published in
*Child's Calendar Beautiful*, 1905

The alder by the river
Shakes out her powdery curls;
The willow buds in silver
For little boys and girls.

The little birds fly over,
And oh how sweet they sing,
To tell the happy children
That once again 'tis spring.

The gay green grass comes creeping
So soft beneath their feet;
The frogs begin to ripple
A music clear and sweet.

And buttercups are coming
And scarlet columbine
And in the sunny meadows
The dandelions shine.

And just as many daisies
As their soft hands can hold.
The little ones may gather
All fair in white and gold.

Here blows the warm red clover,
There peeps the violet blue;
Oh, happy little children,
God made them all for you.

"The Soul can hear the violets grow; it can hear the throbbing heart of God." – Edwin Leibfreed

## MAY IN BLOOM
Helen Maring (1900-1986), published in
"Magnificat" magazine, 1941

May is so beautiful:
Orchards are fair;
Branches of fruit trees
Make gardens of air.

Flowers of fragrance
Bloom in the light;
Fall like the snowflakes
Showering white.

Orchards of heaven
Grow with a grace,
And like a blessing
Perfume the place.

Each tree in blossom,
Each lovely spray,
In this month of Our Lady,
Bring glory to May.

"Most young people find botany a dull study. So it is,
as taught from the text-books in the schools; but study
it yourself in the fields and woods, and you will find it a
source of perennial delight." – John Burroughs

May 13 – Our Lady of Fatima
and Blessed Imelda Lambertini

## MAIDEN MOTHER, MEEK AND MILD
Published in *Catholic Hymns*, 1860

Maiden Mother, meek and mild,
Take, oh! Take me for thy child;
All my life, oh! Let it be
My best joy to think of thee.

When my eyes are closed in sleep,
Through the night my slumbers keep;
Make my latest thought to be
How to love thy Son and thee.

Teach me, when the sunbeam bright
Calls me with its golden light,
How my waking thoughts may be
Turned to Jesus and to thee.

## BLESSED IMELDA
Published in *American Cardinal Reader:
Book* 2, 1929

Imelda's little heart was free from sin.

How glad she was when Jesus entered in!
And so I pray that my heart, too, will be
As pure as hers, when Jesus comes to me.

"Give me the splendid silent sun with all his beams
full-dazzling." – Walt Whitman

## Rain

Daniel A. Lord (1888-1955), published in
*Chants for Children*, 1942

Since rain is good for crops in May,

The farmers bless a rainy day.
But so do I. Thank God who made
The puddles where a child can wade.

## Because He Loves Us
## (From "January")

Alice Cary (1820-1871), published in *The Poetical Works
of Alice and Phoebe Cary*, 1892

We tread through fields of speckled flowers

As if we did not know
Our Father made them beautiful
Because He loves us so.

"Nature, like an enthusiastic gardener, could not resist
the temptation to plant flowers everywhere."
John Muir

## THE WASP AND THE BEE
Jane Taylor (1783-1824, published in
*Rhymes for the Nursery*, 1831

A wasp met a bee that was just buzzing by,
And he said, little cousin, can you tell me why
You are loved so much better by people than I?

My back shines as bright and as yellow as gold,
And my shape is most elegant too, to behold;
Yet nobody likes me for that I am told.

Ah! cousin, the bee said, 'tis all very true.
But if I were half as much mischief to do,
Indeed they would love me no better than you.

You have a fine shape and a delicate wing,
They own you are handsome, but there is one thing
They cannot put up with, and that is your sting.

My coat is quite homely and plain, as you see,
Yet nobody ever is angry with me,
Because I'm a humble and innocent bee.

From this little story, let people beware,
Because, like the wasp, if ill-natured they are,
They will never be loved, if they're ever so fair.

"The whole realm of nature is meant, I believe,
to *speak to us*, to teach us lessons in parables—to
lead our hearts upward to God who made us and
fitted us also for our special place in creation."
Elizabeth Brightwen

## An Apple Orchard in the Spring
William Martin (died 1913), published in
*The Book of Easter*, 1910

. . . Have you plucked the apple blossoms in the
spring?
In the spring?
And caught their subtle odors in the spring?
Pink buds pouting at the light,
Crumpled petals baby white,
Just to touch them a delight—
In the spring.

Have you walked beneath the apple blossoms in the
spring?
In the spring?
Beneath the apple blossoms in the spring?
When the pink cascades are falling,
And the silver brooklets brawling,
And the cuckoo bird soft calling
In the spring.

If you have not, then you know not, in the spring,
In the spring,
Half the color, beauty, wonder of the spring.
No sweet sight can I remember,
Half so precious, half so tender,
As the apple blossoms render
In the spring.

"And as I looked a quickening gust
Of wind blew up to me and thrust
Into my face a miracle
Of orchard-breath, and with the smell,—
I know not how such things can be!—
I breathed my soul back into me."
Edna St. Vincent Millay, "Renascence"

## SAINT PASCHAL BAYLON
## (PATRON OF THE HOLY EUCHARIST)
Hyacinth Blocker (1904-1969), published in
*Locust Bloom and Other Poems*, 1938

Only a simple shepherd-boy
Unlettered, dull and poor was he,
And yet he daily felt a joy
Denied to men like you and me;
For as the lambs he walked among
His heart was pure and free and young.

Only a simple brown-robed Friar,
With kitchen chores his daily task,
And yet he scaled a loftier spire
Of grace than we would even ask;
For still his shepherd ways he trod—
He shephereded the Lamb of God!

"Walk with your feet on earth, but in your heart,
be in heaven." – St. John Bosco

## GRASS

Edgar Fawcett (1847-1904), published in
*Songs of Doubt and Dream*, 1891

We say of the oak, "How grand of girth!"
 Of the willow we say, "How slender!"
And yet to the soft grass clothing the earth
 How slight is the praise we render.

But the grass knows well in her secret heart,
 How we love her cool green raiment*!
So she plays in silence her lovely part,
 And care not at all for payment.


\* clothing

"For from the greatness and the beauty of created
things their original author, by analogy, is seen."
Wisdom 13:5

## MAY NIGHT
Sara Teasdale (1884-1933), published in
*Rivers to the Sea*, 1915

The spring is fresh and fearless
And every leaf is new,
The world is brimmed with moonlight,
The lilac brimmed with dew.

Here in the moving shadows
I catch my breath and sing—
My heart is fresh and fearless
And over-brimmed with spring.

"Reverence for the created world is surely a
mark of sanctity." – Wayne Simsic, *Natural Prayer*

## WHERE GO THE BOATS?
Robert Louis Stevenson (1850–1894), published in
*A Child's Garden of Verse*, 1885

Dark brown is the river.

Golden is the sand.
It flows along for ever,
With trees on either hand.

Green leaves a-floating,
Castles of the foam,
Boats of mine a-boating—
Where will all come home?

On goes the river
And out past the mill,
Away down the valley,
Away down the hill.

Away down the river,
A hundred miles or more,
Other little children
Shall bring my boats ashore.

"Sometimes, if you stand on the bottom rail of a
bridge and lean over to watch the river slipping slowly
away beneath you, you will suddenly know everything
there is to be known." – A. A. Milne, *The House at
Pooh Corner*

## THE ROOKS
Jane Euphemia Browne (1811-1898), published in
*Easy Poetry for Children*, 1866

The rooks are building on the trees;
They build there every spring.
"Caw, caw," is all they say,
For none of them can sing.

They're up before the break of day,
And up till late at night;
For they must labor busily
As long as it is light.

And many a crooked stick they bring,
And many a slender twig,
And many a tuft of moss, until
Their nests are round and big.

"Caw, caw!" Oh, what a noise
They make in rainy weather!
Good children always speak by turns,
But rooks all talk together.

"To strong, susceptible characters, the music of
nature is not confined to sweet sounds."
John Burroughs

## SAINT RITA

Sister Mary Josita Belger (1899-1978), published in
*Sing a Song of Holy Things*, 1945

Saint Rita's holy feast day
Comes in the month of May,
When valley lilies ring their bells,
And grass is green and gay.

She loved her suffering Lord so much
That on her snow white brow
A mark of thorn appeared one day,
And no one knew just how.

It was a sign of God's great love
For Rita always tried
To do the better thing for love
Of Jesus crucified.

Now we pray to this dear saint
In time of greatest need.
Our Savior can't forget her,
But will answer her indeed.

"Weaving a crown out of thorns, they placed it on his
head, and a reed in his right hand. And kneeling
before him, they mocked him, saying, 'Hail, King of
the Jews!'" – Matthew 27:29

## THE RAINBOW FAIRIES
Lissie M. Hadley, published in
*Child's Calendar Beautiful*, 1905

Two little clouds one summer day
   Went flying through the sky.
They went so fast they bumped their heads.
   And both began to cry.
Old Father Sun looked out and said,
   "O, never mind, my dears,
I'll send my little fairy folk
   To dry your falling tears."
One fairy came in violet,
   And one in indigo.
In blue, green, orange, red,—
   They made a pretty row.
They wiped the cloud tears all away,
   And then from out the sky
Upon a line the sunbeam made
   They hung their gowns to dry.

## THE BUTTERFLY
John B. Tabb, published in *Poems of the English Race*,
1921

Leafless, stemless, floating flower,
From a rainbow's scattered bower,
Like a bubble of the air
Blown by fairies, tell me where
Seed or action I may find
Bearing blossoms of thy kind.

"Try to be a rainbow in someone's cloud."
Maya Angelou

## A FANCY

Ninette M. Lowster, published in
*The Western Teacher: Volume 13*, 1904

The flowers are Nature's poems
    In blue and red and gold;
With every change from bud to bloom
    Sweet fantasies unfold.

The trees are Nature's music—
    Her living harps are they,
On which the fingers of the wind
    Majestic marches play.

## HONEYSUCKLE

Lucy Wheelock, published in *Arbor Day Manual*, 1890

I am the honeysuckle,
    With my drooping head;
And early in the spring time
    I don my dress of red.
I grow in quiet woodlands.
    Beneath some budding tree;

**So when you take a ramble**

    Just look for me.

"Man has created some lovely dwellings . . . But he
has not . . . created a substitute for a sunset, a grove
of pines, the music of the winds, the dank smell of the
deep forest, or the shy beauty of a wildflower."
Harvey Broome

## FERN SONG

Fr. John Bannister Tabb (1845-1909), published in
*A Selection from the Verses of John B. Tabb,* 1909

Dance to the beat of the rain, little Fern,

And spread out your palms again,
And say, "Tho' the sun
Has my vesture spun
He has labored, alas, in vain,
But for the shade
That the Cloud has made
And the gift of the Dew and the Rain."
Then laugh and upturn
All your fronds, little Fern,
And rejoice in the beat of the rain.

"Study nature, love nature, stay close to nature.
It will never fail you." – Frank Lloyd Wright

## ST. PHILIP NERI
Robert Hugh Benson (1871-1914), published in
*An Alphabet of Saints*, 1906

**"P"** is good ST. PHILIP NERI, friend of all the
friends of Rome;
He was eighteen when he chose the Holy City for his
home;
There he lived the life of hermits, eating little else but
bread,
In one tiny little room in which he never had a bed.
PHILIP had the gifts and graces of St. PETER and St.
PAUL,
And the Romans turned to piety and penance at his call,
While the numberless young people who sought PHILIP
for advice
Said his humble little room was like an earthly Paradise.
He longed to die for CHRIST, as in the Catacomb he
prayed
At the grave in which the Martyr, St. SEBASTIAN, was
laid;
A Martyr's death is glorious, but PHILIP has the glory
Of founding a great Congregation, called the Oratory.
    If I told you half the holy things that PHILIP did and
        said,
    I should have to end the Alphabet with "P" instead
        of " Z."

"He who wishes for anything but Christ does not know
what he wishes; he who asks for anything but Christ,
does not know what he is asking; he who works, and
not for Christ, does not know what he is doing."
St. Philip Neri

## WHEN WOODS AWAKE
Old English Ballad, published in
*My Book House: In the Nursery*, 1954

When woods awake and trees are green
And leaves are large and long,
'Tis merry to walk in the forest fair
And hear the small birds' song.

## WHAT DOES LITTLE BIRDIE SAY
Alfred Tennyson (1809-1892), published in
*Tennyson for the Young*, 1891

What does little birdie say
In her nest at peep of day?
Let me fly, says little birdie,
Mother, let me fly away.
Birdie, rest a little longer,
Till the little wings are stronger,
So she rests a little longer,
Then she flies away. . . .

"As soon as he is able to keep it himself, a nature-diary is a source of delight to a child. Every day's walk gives him something to enter . . ." – Charlotte Mason

## THE LITTLE POET
Eben E. Rexford, published in
*Primary Education: Volume 2*, 1894

Out in the garden wee Elsie
   Was gathering flowers for me;
"O mamma!" she cried, "Hurry, hurry,
   Here's something I want you to see."
I went to the window. Before her
   A velvet-winged butterfly flew,
And the pansies themselves were not brighter
   Than the beautiful creature in hue.

"Oh! Isn't it pretty!" cried Elsie,
   With eager and wondering eyes,
As she watched it soar lazily upward
   Against the soft blue of the skies.
"I know what it is, don't you, mamma?"
   Oh! The burden of these little things
When the soul of a poet is in them,
   "It's a pansy—a pansy with wings."

"Happiness is like a butterfly, the more you chase it,
the more it will evade you, but if you notice the other
things around you, it will gently come and sit on your
shoulder." – Henry David Thoreau

## THE DAISIES
Sister Margaret Patrice, published in
*A Lovely Gate Set Wide*, 1946

The daisies of the grassy hills,

With golden faces, lacy frills,
Are sent by God to bring us cheer
And deck the fields of May each year.

The whole year long they'd like to stay
And play in the meadows clear;
But when God says, "Come, come, my dear"
Each folds her snow-white shawl away.

When I am called indoors from play
And Mother says, "Put toys away,"
I'll quickly do what I am told
And will not stop to pout or scold.

"I still feel the profound and poetic impressions which
were born in my soul at the sight of fields enameled
with corn-flowers and all types of wild flowers. Already
I was in love with the wide-open spaces."
St. Therese, *The Story of a Soul*

## CLOVERS
Helena Leeming Jelliffe (1868-1916), published in
*Songs of the Tree-top and Meadow*, 1899

The clovers have no time to play;
They feed the cows and make the hay,

And trim the lawns, and help the bees,
Until the sun sinks through the trees.

And then they lay aside their cares,
And fold their hands to say their prayers,

And drop their tired little heads
And go to sleep in clover beds.

And when the day dawns clear and blue
They wake and wash their hands in dew;

And as the sun climbs up the sky,
They hold them up and let them dry.

And then to work the whole long day,
For clovers have no time to play.

"To make a prairie it takes a clover and one bee,
One clover, and a bee.
And revery.
The revery alone will do,
If bees are few."
Emily Dickinson, "To Make a Prairie (1755)"

## THE HAIL MARY

Marigold Hunt (1905-1994), published in
*Gospel Rhymes*, 1947

Our Lady had a cousin
Who was getting rather old,
Her name was St. Elizabeth
And she was as good as gold.

Our Lady loved Elizabeth,
So God let her see
Who Our Lady was, and whose
Mother she would be.

*"Blessed art thou among women,"*
St. Elizabeth said,
*"And blessed the fruit of thy womb,
Jesus."* Bow your head.

An angel and a saint
Showed us the way
We should greet Our Lady
And what we should say.

"Mary set out and traveled to the hill country in haste
to a town of Judah, where she entered the house of
Zechariah and greeted Elizabeth. When Elizabeth
heard Mary's greeting, the infant leaped in her
womb, and Elizabeth, filled with the holy Spirit, cried
out in a loud voice and said, 'Most blessed are you
among women, and blessed is the fruit of your womb.'"
Luke 1:39-42

# HOLY DAYS AND HOLIDAYS

Arbor Day
Last Friday in April

## TREES

Abbie Farwell Brown (1871-1927), published in
*Star Jewels and Other Wonders*, 1905

However little I may be,
At least I, too, can plant a tree.

And some day it will grow so high
That it can whisper to the sky,

And spread its leafy branches wide
To make a shade on every side;

Then on a sultry summer day,
The people resting there will say,—

"Oh, good and wise and great was he
Who thought to plant this blessed tree!"

.

An excellent read for this holiday for older readers
is Sue Alexander's *Behold the Trees* picture book.

## AMERICA
Samuel Francis Smith (1808-1895), written in 1831

My country, 'tis of Thee,
Sweet Land of Liberty
Of thee I sing;
Land where my fathers died,
Land of the pilgrims' pride,
From every mountain side
Let Freedom ring.

My native country, thee,
Land of the noble free,
Thy name I love;
I love thy rocks and rills,
Thy woods and templed hills,
My heart with rapture thrills
Like that above.

Our fathers' God to Thee,
Author of Liberty,
To thee we sing,
Long may our land be bright
With Freedom's holy light,
Protect us by thy might
Great God, our King.

## FIRST COMMUNION DAY
Published in *A Book of Sanctity*

Side by side we're kneeling
On our First Communion Day.
The air is fresh and lovely
The songs and flowers gay.

The candles on the altar
And the little golden bell
Join us in our happiness
And try our joy to tell.

Angels are around us—
I can almost feel them near.
The Saints and Mother Mary
Are surely present here.

Help me, Mother Mary,
Welcome Jesus to my heart.
Tell Him that I love Him
And help me do my part.

## HOLY COMMUNION
### T. V. Nicholas, published in *Gospel Rhymes*, 1947

Once Jesus told His people that the time would soon
  arrive
When He Himself should be their Food to keep their
  souls alive;
But many walked no more with Him; they said, "This
  can't be true,"
When He spoke about Communion for themselves and
    me and you.

Now if Jesus hadn't meant it He'd have hastened to
  explain
That they hadn't understood Him and must all come
  back again,
But, just because He meant it so, He couldn't bid them
  stay;
But He said to His Apostles, "Will you also go away?"

Of course Saint Peter showed Him that they didn't
  mean to go,
But wasn't it a pity that the others acted so?
That when His solemn promise of the Bread of Life they
  heard
His very own disciples should refuse to take His word?

*Dear Lord, I often wonder where those poor disciples*
  *went,*
*And if some of them were sorry and you helped them to*
  *repent;*
*I'll pray for those disciples on my next Communion Day,*
*For anyone who doubts Your Word and all who keep away.*

## MOTHERS

Rev. Hugh F. Blunt (1877-1957), published in
*A Lovely Gate Set Wide*, 1946

"Mothers have a way with them
Only mothers know:
Just a secret heavenly
God has taught them so.

Arms that know the way to make
Softest cradle bed,
Giving shelter from the world
To a baby's head.

Mothers have a way with them
Only mothers know,
For to take His place on earth
God just made them so."

## ONLY ONE

George Cooper, published in
*An American Anthology*, 1900

Hundreds of stars in the pretty sky;
    Hundreds of shells on the shore together;
Hundreds of birds that go singing by;
    Hundreds of bees in the sunny weather.

Hundreds of dewdrops to greet the dawn;
    Hundreds of lambs in the purple clover;
Hundreds of butterflies on the lawn;
    But only one mother the wide world over.

## MY MOTHER MARY

Sister Mary Josita Belger (1899-1978), published in
*Sing a Song of Holy Things*, 1945

When I think of Mother Mary,
And her soul of purest white,
I pray to her to keep me
Always in her sight.

From early dawn she watches,
As I walk along the way.
She smiles with joy to see me
Doing good from day to day.

Each night when darkness gathers,
And I'm a sleepy-head,
My Mother watches always
Beside my little bed.

I'll pray to Mary daily,
And she will be my friend.
She will take me straight to Jesus
When life comes to an end.

## FLOWER AND WEED
Elvira S. Miller (1824-1907), published in
*Religious Poems for Little Folks*, 1936

Unto our Lady's altar,
Two little children came;
High through the painted casement
The sun shone like a flame;
Outside the birds were singing,
The day was nearly gone,
And there, like frozen music,
Our Mother's statue shone.

One bore the rarest roses
Culled from the hothouse store
And one some tiny posies—
Just common weeds, no more.
And where the gorgeous blossoms
Shone in a rosy drift,
Warm from his timid fingers,
The poor child laid his gift.

That night a radiant vision
Came down from angel land;
Our Lady smiled upon him, and the weeds were in
her hand;
And he knew then not the offering
Of treasures rare and fine,
But the love he gave her with it
Had made his gift divine.

# MEMORIAL DAY

Annette Wynne (died 1953), published in
*For Days and Days*, 1919

Is it enough to think today
Of all our brave, then put away
The thought until a year has sped?
Is this full honor for our dead?

Is it enough to sing a song
And deck a grave; and all year long
Forget the brave who died that we
Might keep our great land proud and free?

Full service needs a greater toll—
That we who live give heart and soul
To keep the land they died to save,
And be ourselves, in turn, the brave!

# ASH WEDNESDAY, LENT, EASTER, AND BEYOND

## ASH WEDNESDAY (1862)

Fr. Abram Joseph Ryan (1838-1886), published in
*War Lyrics and Songs of the South*, 1866

The six weeks' Sabbath has begun;
A little while, my soul be done
With heat and flurry of life's race;
Take time to cultivate God's grace.

Most of the seeds He sowed are lost,
Those that are left are passion-tost:
Save them, heart, ere it be too late;
Redeem them from pride, scorn, and hate. . . .

Thy Father knows is best for thee:
Trust Him, for farther He can see
Than thou. Think of thy love-marked past—
Easter comes after Lenten fast. . . .

## WISHING
Ella Wheeler Wilcox (1855-1919), published in
*Poems of Power*, 1902

Do you wish the world were better?
Let me tell you what to do:
Set a watch upon your actions,
Keep them always straight and true;
Let your thoughts be clean and high:
Of the sphere you occupy.

Do you wish the world was wiser?
Well, suppose you make a start
By accumulating wisdom
In the scrapbook of your heart.
Do not waste one page on folly;
Live to learn, and learn to live.
If you want to give men knowledge
You must get it ere you give.

Do you wish the world were happy?
Then remember day by day
Just to scatter seeds of kindness
As you pass along the way:
For the pleasures of many
May be oft times traced to one,
As the hand that plants an acorn
Shelters armies from the sun.

## THE CATHOLIC CHILD

Sister Mary Josita Belger (1899-1978), published in
*Sing a Song of Holy Things*, 1945

A good and holy child of God
A child of Mother Church
Is known by how he acts each day
You need not stop to search.

He goes to Mass on Sundays
And all the Holy Days,
And shows that he is serving God
In many little ways.

He eats no meat on Fridays,
But takes a fish instead.
He gives up for his Savior,
And still he is well fed.

He loves the holy sacraments—
Confession for his sins,
Communion with his Savior
Heaven's joy on earth begins.

You always know a child of God,
He's happy as can be.
Because he keeps the holy law
Of Mother Church, you see.

## AFTER A VISIT TO THE BLESSED SACRAMENT
S.M. St. John, published in
*Religious Poems for Little Folks*, 1936

Whenever in pain or sin,

I love to enter in
Before some altar door,
God's favor to implore.

We talk a little while—
A word or two, a smile,
His love's absolving kiss,
Such reverential bliss!

And then with clearer ken
I face life's ways again;
'Mid all its deafening roar,
King of my soul once more!

## GOD'S GREATNESS
Sister Mary Josita Belger (1899-1978), published in
*Sing a Song of Holy Things*, 1945

Dear God, I know You're everywhere
No matter where I go, you're there.

If I could fly above the sky,
Your throne would be there built on high.

And if I dig down in the ground,
Even there You're to be found.

Wherever there's a single space
The angels see You face to face.

But I can't see You till I die—
No matter how hard I may try.

For You are spirit; You can see,
And know all things—yes, even me.

You know my thoughts, my words, my deeds,
Your loving eye sees all my needs.

There's nothing hard for You to do;
To make a world is fun for You.

You take the good to heaven bright,
And punish evil with Your might.

But You are patient, kind, and true
To sinners who come back to You.

Your holiness I now adore,
Oh, make me love You more and more.

## MORNING PRAYER
Fr. John C. Rath (1910-2007), published in
*Religious Poems for Little Folks*, 1936

Jesus, your child returns to You

The many thanks that are Your due;
All that I think, or do, or say
Give praise to you throughout the day.

Angel of God, your vigil kept
Beside my bed, the while I slept;
Keep me from sin and guide aright
that I may follow pathways bright.

Mother of God, forever true,
Your little one now calls on you;
Grant me to live like your dear Son,
To be with you when life is done. Amen.

## A SIMPLE RECIPE

James Whitcomb Riley (1849-1916), published in
*Joyful Poems for Children*, 1892

To be a wholly worthy man,
As you, my boy, would like to be,—
This is to show you how you can—
This simple recipe:

Be honest—both in word and act,
Be strictly truthful through and through:
Fact cannot fail. You stick to fact,
And fact will stick to you.

Be clean—outside and in, and sweep
Both hearth and heart and hold them bright;
Wear snowy linen—aye, and keep
Your *conscience* snowy-white.

Do right, your utmost—good *must come*
To you who do your level-best—
Your very hopes will help you some,
And work will do the rest.

## HYMN TO THE HOLY CHILD JESUS
Published in *Pleadings of the Soul*, 1895

Jesus, teach me how to pray,
Suffer not my thoughts to stray,
Send distractions far away,
Sweet Holy Child.

Let me not be rude or wild,
Make me humble, meek, and mild,
Pure as angels undefiled,
Sweet Holy Child.

When I work, or when I play,
Be Thou with me through the day,
Teach me what to do and say,
Sweet Holy Child.

Make me love Thy Mother blest,
Safe beneath her care to rest,
As a bird within its nest,
Sweet Holy Child.

## LITTLE THINGS
Julia Fletcher Carney (1823-1908),
published in *The Home Book of Verse*, 1915

Little drops of water,
Little grains of sand,
Make the mighty ocean
And the pleasant land.

Thus the little minutes
Humble though they be,
Make the mighty ages
Of eternity.

Thus our little errors
Lead the soul away
From the path of virtue
Off in sin to stray.

## THE WAY OF THE CROSS

Leonard Feeney (1897-1978), published in
*In Towns and Little Towns*, 1927

Along the dark aisles
Of a chapel dim,
The little lame girl
Drags her withered limb.

And all alone she searches
The shadows on the walls
To find the three pictures
Where Jesus falls.

## WHAT GOD HATH MADE

William Bourne Oliver Peabody (1799-1847), published
in *Bancroft's First-Fifth Reader: Book 3*, 1883

God made the sun, and gave him light;

He made the moon to shine by night;
He placed the brilliant stars on high,
And leads them through the midnight sky.

He made the earth in order stand;
He made the ocean and the land;
He made the hills their places know,
And gentle rivers round them flow.

He made the forests, and sustains
The grass that clothes the field and plains;
He sends from heaven the summer showers,
And makes the meadows bright with flowers.

He made the living things; with care
He feeds the wanderers of the air;
He gave the beasts their dens and caves,
And fish, their dwelling in the waves.

He called all beings into birth
That crowd the ocean, air, and earth;
And all in heaven and earth proclaim
The glory of His holy name.

## LOVE AT HOME

Sister Mary Josita Belger (1899-1978),
published in *Sing a Song of Holy Things*, 1945

Home is a very happy place
When all begin the day
With prayer to ask God's blessing
And help along the way,

When children honor, love, obey,
And share their every toy,
Are always kind in thought and deed
And give their parents joy.

When all the family kneel at night
To say an evening prayer,
To thank God for His blessings
And for His loving care.

Such homes are lovely gardens
Where God can walk each day,
Where flowers give sweet perfumes
Along the Master's way.

## DO NOT LOOK FOR WRONG OR EVIL
Alice Cary (1820-1871), published in *The Poetical Works of Alice and Phoebe Cary*, 1884

**D**o *not look for wrong and evil—*
You will find them if you do;
As you measure for your neighbor
He will measure back to you.

Look for goodness, look for gladness,
You will meet them all the while;
If you bring a smiling visage
To the glass, you meet a smile.

## THE HIGHEST GOOD

James Whitcomb Riley (1849-1916),
published in *Joyful Poems for Children*, 1892

To attain the highest good

Of true man and womanhood,
Simply do your honest best—
God with joy will do the rest.

## TRY AGAIN

William Hickson (1803-1870), published in "Supplement
to the Courant: Volume 6," 1840

'T is a lesson you should heed—
 Try again;
If at first you don't succeed,
 Try again.
Then your courage should appear;
For if you will persevere,
You will conquer, never fear,
 Try again.

Once or twice though you should fail,
If you would at last prevail,
 Try again.
If we strive, 'tis no disgrace
Though we did not win the race—
What should you do in that case?
 Try again.

If you find your task is hard.
 Try again;
Time will bring you your reward,
 Try again;
All that other folk can do,
Why with patience should not you?
Only keep this rule in view,
 Try again.

## GOD'S HOME [ADAPTED]
Rev. Edward F. Garesche (1876-1960), published in
*The Four Gates*, 1913

"Mother, where does Jesus dwell?"
Child, He dwells everywhere,
In the earth and in the air,
In the wide, unending blue—
Even on the farthest star,
Where creation's lights are,
Past all ken* of me and you!

"Mother, has He any home?"
First, His home's in heaven bright,
Wondrous mansions, built of light;
Then, the tabernacle blest;
But the home He loves the most,
More than heaven or Sacred Host,
Is your sinless, loving breast!


*range of knowledge; understanding

## .HOW TO BE HAPPY
Published in *Child's Calendar Beautiful*, 1905

Are you cross and disgusted, my dear little man?
  I will tell you a wonderful trick
That will bring you contentment if anything can:
    Do something for somebody—quick!
    Do something for somebody—quick!

Are you very tired with play, little girl?
    Weary, discouraged, and sick?
I'll tell you the loveliest game in the world—
    Do something for somebody—quick!
    Do something for somebody—quick!

Though it rain like the rain of the floods, little man,
    And the clouds are forbidding and thick,
You can make the sun shine in your soul, little
man—
    Do something for somebody—quick!
    Do something for somebody—quick!

Though the skies are like brass overhead, little girl,
    And the walk like a well-heated brick;
And are all your affairs in a terrible whirl?
    Do something for somebody—quick!
        Do something for somebody—quick!

## OBEDIENCE

Phoebe Cary (1824-1871), published in *The Poetical Works of Alice and Phoebe Cary*, 1884

If you're told to do a thing,

And mean to do it really;
Never let it be by halves;
Do it fully, freely!

Do not make a poor excuse,
Waiting, weak, unsteady;
All obedience worth the name,
Must be prompt and ready.

## THE TEN COMMANDMENTS
Sister Mary Josita Belger (1899-1978), published in
*Sing a Song of Holy Things*, 1945

The First Commandment says that I should pray to
God alone.
And love Him more than anything I think, or see, or own.
The Second one commands us all to bless the Holy Name,
Not speak It when we're angry, not in fun—'twould be a
shame.
The Third Commandment tells us all to keep the Lord's
day well,
To go to Mass, to do kind acts, and other prayers to tell.
The Fourth reminds us all to love our parents and obey,
That God may bless us while on earth in every little way.
The Fifth Commandment tells us we must not kill anyone,
Not harm a person any way, no matter how it's done.
The Sixth and Ninth Commandments tells us always to
be pure,
And then we'll all be happy and will make our heaven
secure.
The Seventh says we may not steal from any one at all,
And if we borrow, give it back—a crayon or a ball.
The Eighth Commandment warns that we should never
tell a lie,
Nor say mean things of others, though they have made
us cry.
And by the Tenth and last command God wants us all to
be
Happy with what we have and own, not wishing all we see.
And if we keep these ten commands that God gave us on
stone,
We show Him that we want to live for Him, for Him alone.

## GOD'S HELP

Sister Mary Josita Belger (1899-1978), published in
*Sing a Song of Holy Things*, 1945

God is very near each day,
So when I work or when I play
I say, "My Jesus, help!"

Just as soon as I awake,
And promise things for His dear sake,
I add, "My Jesus, help!"

Whenever hard things come my way,
I always stop and quickly say,
"My Lord, my Jesus, help!"

Jesus hears me when I call;
He gives His helping grace to all
Who say, "My Jesus help!"

## EVERY DAY

Felix Mendelssohn (1809-1847),
published in *Stories of Great Musicians*, 1905

L ove the beautiful,

Seek out the true,
Wish for the good,
And the best do!

(See Philippians 4:8.)

## DON'T GIVE UP

Phoebe Cary (1824-1871), published in *The Poetical Works of Alice and Phoebe Cary*, 1884

If you've tried and have not won,
Never stop for crying;
All that's great and good is done
Just by patient trying.

Though young birds, in flying, fall,
Still their wings grow stronger;
And the next time they can keep
Up a little longer.

Though the sturdy oak has known
Many a blast that bowed her,
She has risen again, and grown
Loftier and prouder.

If by easy work you beat,
Who the more will prize you?
Gaining victory from defeat,
That's the test that tries you!

## FIRST STATION
## JESUS IS ORDERED TO DIE

Sister Mary Josita Belger (1899-1978), published in
*Sing a Song of Holy Things*, 1945

O h, Jesus, when I see You stand
Before those wicked men,
I wish that I could speak for You,
And make You free again.

If Pilate had been strong and brave
And had not feared their power,
He would have told them You were good
And helped You in that hour.

But, Jesus dear, I, too, have stood
Among the rough, mean crowd.
I, too, have loved the things of earth
Far more than you, my God.

Oh, mercy, please, my Savior dear,
I only ask of You
That I may make up for my sins,
And win Your graces, too.

## SECOND STATION
## JESUS TAKES HIS CROSS
Sister Mary Josita Belger (1899-1978), published in
*Sing a Song of Holy Things*, 1945

O h, Jesus, taking now your cross
With loving, trembling arms,
Where is all Your beauty gone?
Where are all your charms?

You've suffered through the dark, cold night,
And now when it is day,
You take the cross, the heavy wood,
And walk up Calvary's way.

Daily, Lord, You ask Your child
To take the cross with love,
And follow in your blessed steps
That lead to you above.

But, oh, how different I am!
How very mean and small.
Now may I learn to bear my cross
For You I'll suffer all.

## THIRD STATION
## JESUS FALLS THE FIRST TIME
Sister Mary Josita Belger (1899-1978), published in
*Sing a Song of Holy Things*, 1945

O h, Jesus, fallen on the ground,
Beneath that heavy load,
It makes me sad to see You lie
In suffering on the road.

The wicked soldiers pull You on.
They drive You all the way.
To save this little soul of mine,
Oh, what a price You pay!

I often stumble with my cross,
Though it is very small,
The little things that come each day,
A pain, a loss, a fall.

Oh, dearest Jesus, love me still,
And help me with Your grace,
To do Your will, and through each day,
Your holy steps to trace.

## FOURTH STATION
## JESUS MEETS HIS MOTHER

Sister Mary Josita Belger (1899-1978), published in
*Sing a Song of Holy Things*, 1945

Jesus, when Your loving eyes
Looked on Your Mother's face
Your suffering heart wept silently,
To see her in that place.

She was filled with holy thoughts,
With love of God alone,
But a Mother's love and pity
In her sad eyes shone.

Help me to comfort her, dear Lord,
By being good and kind
To all the sorry folk I meet,
The sick, and poor, and blind.

Help me think of others more,
And think of self much less.
Make me like Your Mother, Lord,
In grace and holiness.

## FIFTH STATION
## SIMON HELPS JESUS CARRY HIS CROSS
Sister Mary Josita Belger (1899-1978), published in
*Sing a Song of Holy Things*, 1945

My Jesus, many blessings came
To Simon of Cyrene,
Who helped You with the heavy cross.
At first he would not lean

The shameful wood upon his back
To serve his suffering Lord.
But as he helped his heart grew glad,
And great was his reward.

My life, too, will be happy
If I try to please my Lord,
By helping other boys and girls
In thought and deed and word.

I turn to You, my Jesus,
And promise every day,
To help someone come close to You
By all I do and say.

## SIXTH STATION
## VERONICA WIPES THE FACE OF JESUS
Sister Mary Josita Belger (1899-1978), published in
*Sing a Song of Holy Things*, 1945

O h, Jesus, when Your holy face
Was on the white cloth drawn
How happy was Veronica
As she looked sadly on

The picture of her suffering Lord,
Painted clear and true.
She dared the angry passing crowd
To show her love for You.

Your picture, Lord, should also be
Pressed deep in my poor soul.
To grow more like You every day
Will be my only goal.

Forgive me, Jesus, all my sins
And let me see Your face
Wiped clean of all its suffering
When I have grown in grace.

## SEVENTH STATION
## JESUS FALLS THE SECOND TIME
Sister Mary Josita Belger (1899-1978), published in
*Sing a Song of Holy Things*, 1945

You ou fell a second time, dear Lord,
On that sad, holy day,
As You climbed up the stony hill
Along Mount Calvary way.

You were God, as well as man,
But hid Your power divine,
And as a man You suffered
To save this soul of mine.

I know I have been naughty, Lord,
I have not even tried
To raise my heart above the earth
To You Who for me died.

Oh, Jesus, I am sorry
I've been naughty in the past.
Please help me spend my little life
More close to You, at last.

## EIGHTH STATION
## JESUS COMFORTS THE WOMEN
Sister Mary Josita Belger (1899-1978), published in
*Sing a Song of Holy Things,* 1945

The women of Jerusalem
Came crying down the road,
And met You, dearest, Jesus,
With the cross, that heavy load.

They spoke soft words of pity,
And whispered thanks to You.
The tiny babies in their arms,
For You were crying, too.

"Weep not for Me, but for yourselves,"
You told them sorrily,
"For yourselves and your children,
Now weep, but not for Me."

I, too, must weep for my sins, Lord,
That cause You bitter pain.
I'll do my best to love You now,
And keep my soul from stain.

## NINTH STATION
## JESUS FALLS THE THIRD TIME
Sister Mary Josita Belger (1899-1978), published in
*Sing a Song of Holy Things*, 1945

My Jesus, once again you fell
On Calvary's holy hill.
Weak and worn with suffering
You walked along until

The cross upon Your shoulder,
Patiently upborne,
Pressed down until the tender flesh
Was bleeding, cut and torn.

Lord Jesus, please forgive my share
Of sin that caused this fall.
I promise every day to watch
My thoughts, my actions all.

I'll help You up, dear Savior,
But not with heavy rope;
I'll raise Your suffering body
With cords of love and hope.

## TENTH STATION
## JESUS IS STRIPPED OF HIS GARMENTS

Sister Mary Josita Belger (1899-1978), published in
*Sing a Song of Holy Things*, 1945

You reach the top of Calvary,
And there they make You stand.
With hurts in every part of You,
In head and feet and hand.

They tear Your clothes off roughly.
The cuts that hurt before
Now make Your holy body feel
And wound and bleeding sore.

Oh, Jesus dear, I bow my head,
And beat my breast in shame,
For I, too, helped those soldiers;
I, too, am to blame.

Not by tearing off Your clothes,
Not by cruel dart,
But by sins of word and deed,
And thought deep in my heart.

## ELEVENTH STATION
## JESUS IS NAILED TO THE CROSS

Sister Mary Josita Belger (1899-1978), published in
*Sing a Song of Holy Things*, 1945

I see them lay You on the cross,
And nail You to the wood.
Three long hours of pain, dear Lord,
You suffered for our good;

Three long hours of prayer for those
Who nailed You to the tree;
Three long hours of suffering
Borne most patiently.

Teach me, dearest Savior,
As on the cross You lie,
To pray for those who hurt me most,
Each day until I die,

To love all men as brothers,
As children of my Lord,
To pray that all may come one day
To heaven's great reward.

## TWELFTH STATION
## JESUS DIES ON THE CROSS
Sister Mary Josita Belger (1899-1978), published in
*Sing a Song of Holy Things,* 1945

And now, dear God, the hour has come
When You will die for me.
What have I done to win Your love,
That You should so love me?

What have I done that You should hang
With tender hands nailed tight,
Those bleeding hands that healed the sick,
That gave the blind their sight.

What have I done that You should hang,
With tender feet all torn,
Those feet that would have walked a world
For one small soul forlorn.

I bow my head in pity, Lord,
As lovingly You die.
I ask Your mercy for my sins,
My sins that crucify.

## THIRTEENTH STATION
## JESUS IS TAKEN DOWN FROM THE CROSS
Sister Mary Josita Belger (1899-1978), published in
*Sing a Song of Holy Things*, 1945

My Savior now has died for me.
His holy head bows low.
Again I say, what have I done
That He should love me so?

As dark night covers all the land,
And earthquake shakes the sod,
A soldier standing says, "Indeed,
This was the Son of God!"

And now my Lord is taken down
And on His Mother's breast
His wounded Head at last can find
All comfort and sweet rest.

Oh, make me, Mother, brave like you,
And always let me feel
The deep pain of your broken heart,
My little soul to heal.

## FOURTEENTH STATION
## JESUS IS LAID IN THE TOMB

Sister Mary Josita Belger (1899-1978), published in
*Sing a Song of Holy Things*, 1945

They take my Savior's body now,
And lay it in the grave.
The same dear Lord Who loved me,
Lies cold within the cave.

They roll the stone before the tomb
And seal my Savior's sleep.
Oh, heavy now their thoughts must be
And loud their hearts must weep.

These friends of His had run away
When trouble came before,
But now with His dear Mother near,
They'll never do it more.

Oh, Mary, let me watch with you
This sad Good Friday night.
Then I, too, will be glad with you,
In Easter's holy light.

## THE GOLDEN CUP

Sister Mary Josita Belger (1899-1978), published in
*Sing a Song of Holy Things*, 1945

I'd like to be the golden cup

Behind the little door
That holds my Savior's Body.
Each day I wish it more.

But soon my heart will hold my God,
As tabernacle shrine,
My heart like sparkling golden cup—
What happiness is mine!

Oh, may my cup, my little heart,
Be filled up to the brim
With thoughts of Jesus all my life,
And burning love for Him.

## SORROW
Marigold Hunt (1905-1994),
published in *Gospel Rhymes*, 1947

Seeds turn into flowers,
Sand turns into glass,
Wheat turns into bread, and bread
Turns into Our Lord at Mass.

Gold turns into money,
Little boys into men
Cream turns into butter—
What about sorrow then?

Nobody could have guessed it
If Our Lord hadn't told—
Sorrow is so precious,
Sorrow is better than gold.

Gold turns into money
But sorrow—turns into joy.
How's that for a thought to comfort
A sad little girl or boy?

Our Lady, highest in Heaven,
Could tell you this is true,
Because of all the heaps of joy
Her sorrow turned into.

## A CHILD'S PRAYER [ADAPTED]

Margaret Betham-Edwards (1836-1919), published in
*The Posy Ring: A Book of Verse for Children*, 1908

God, make my life a little light
  Within the world to glow;
A little flame that burns so bright
  Wherever I may go.

God, make my life a little flower
  That gives great joy to all,
Content to bloom in native bower,
  Although the place be small.

God, make my life a little song
  That gives comfort to the sad,
That helps others to be strong
  And makes the singer glad.

God, make my life a little staff
  Whereon the weak may rest,
And so what health and strength I have
  May serve my neighbors best.

God, make my life a little hymn
  Of tenderness and praise;
Of faith, that never waxes dim,
  In all His wondrous ways.

## THE CHILDREN IN THE TEMPLE
Marigold Hunt (1905-1994), published in
*Gospel Rhymes*, 1947

Our Lord rode into Jerusalem
Among shouting and singing of Psalms,
They covered His path with their Sunday clothes
And big green branches of palms.
*Hosanna to the Son of David!*
The procession stopped at the Temple
And Our Lord went inside,
A crowd of children followed him
And even there they cried:
*Hosanna to the Son of David!*
The Pharisees said, "Really!
What dreadful children these!
Singing in the Temple!
Silence, silence, please!"
*Hosanna to the Son of David!*
The chief priest said, "Certainly,
They should be sent to bed—
Shouting in the Temple!
Did you hear what they said?"
*Hosanna to the Son of David!*
"Yes," said Our Lord, "read
What the Scripture says,
'Our of the mouths of children
Thou has perfected praise!'"
*Hosanna to the Son of David!*

So we sing our loudest,
Very nearly shout,
And thank Our Lord for liking it
In church and out.

## FOUR THINGS

Henry Van Dyke (1852-1933), published in
*Poems: Volume 1*, 1920

Four things a man must learn to do
If he would make his record true:
To think without confusion clearly;
To love his fellow-men sincerely;
To act from honest motives purely;
To trust in God and Heaven securely.

## "I" IS FOR IMMORTALITY
Hilda van Stockum (1908-2006),
published in *Angels' Alphabet*, 1948

Our soul is like a little bird

Homesick for Heaven's skies,
And it will wing its way up there
When death has closed our eyes.

At least, if we have nourished it,
For though the soul can't die
Its wings may slowly waste away
And lose the strength to fly.

## THE WORLD'S BIBLE
### Annie Johnson Flint (1866-1932), published in
### *Leading Light,* 1934

Christ has no hands but our hands to do His work
today;
He has no feet but our feet to lead men in His way;
He has no tongue but our tongues to tell men how He
died;
He has no help but our help to bring them to His side.

We are the only Bible the careless world will read;
We are the sinner's gospel, we are the scoffer's creed;
We are the Lord's last message, given in deed and word;
What if the type is crooked? What if the print is blurred?
What if our hands are busy with other work than His?
What if our feet are walking where sin's allurement is?
What if our tongues are speaking of things His lips would
spurn?
How can we hope to help Him and hasten His return?

## THE AGONY IN THE GARDEN

Sister Mary Josita Belger (1899-1978), published in
*Sing a Song of Holy Things*, 1945

They walked up the hill that evening,
Those sad and lonely friends.
They wanted to stay with their Master
And fight for Him to the end. . . .

He came, and found them sleeping,
Then went, and prayed again,
And asked the Father to keep His Son
From the anger of cruel men.

But the Master gave us a lesson
In the prayer He said in love,
For "Not my will, but Yours be done,"
He prayed to the Father above.

He prayed for His friends who were sleeping,
He prayed for the one who had strayed,
And He prayed for every soul of man
That His tender love had made.

I must follow my Savior's lesson,
And be pleased with the Father's will,
Both when I am young and when I grow old
I must all his words fulfill.

And I, too, must pray for others,
For those who are loving and kind,
And for those who are cruel and mean to me,
For in this I shall happiness find.

## My Turn

Sister Mary Josita Belger (1899-1978), published in
*Sing a Song of Holy Things*, 1945

Oh, how I wish I could have been
Upon that holy hill
When my dear Jesus went alone
To do His Father's will.
The cross was very heavy,
But the soldiers did not care.
They put it over His poor back.
No loving friend was there.
But where were all the children,
He had loved and blessed each day?
Where were the blind, the sick, the poor?
Had they all gone away?
Yes, even Peter, who had said
He would with Jesus die,
Where was he when the soldiers came,
Their Lord to crucify?
He, too, in fear, had run away,
And left his Lord alone.
And Jesus suffered for their sins,
And for my very own.
So when Gods sends a little cross
To show His love for me,
I'll carry it with happiness,
Whatever it may be.
A little pain, a little care
A lesson hard to learn—
I'll offer it to Him, and say,
"Today, dear Lord, my turn."

## THE ANGEL OF THE RESURRECTION
St. Therese of the Child Jesus (1873-1897),
written Christmas 1894

Angel of man's Redeemer, weep no more!

I come with comforts for sad hearts and sore.
This little Child shall gain
   All men's hearts as their King;
He shall arise and reign
   Almighty, triumphing!

. . . I shall roll back the great tomb's rocky door;
   I shall behold His Lovely Face once more;
And I shall sing,
   And I shall then rejoice
When I shall see my King,
   And hear again His voice.

Thy childish eyes, though dim tonight with tears,
   Shall shine with heavenly light throughout the
         eternal years,
O Word of God!
   Thy speech, like burning flame,
Shall sound one day abroad,
   And all Thy love proclaim.

## CHRIST IS RISEN
Sister Mary Josita Belger (1899-1978), published in
*Sing a Song of Holy Things*, 1945

Alleluia! How the earth shook
On that first glad Easter day,
When the Savior rose in glory
Bright as lily bells in May.

Soldiers fell upon their faces,
Filled with fear at that great sight,
And an angel came from heaven,
That the noon day sun more bright.

Yes, an angel told the story—
How he rose up from the dead.
Alleluia! Alleluia!
Rose again as He had said.

# A BALLAD OF EASTER
Theodosia Garrison (1874-1944), published in
*As the Larks Rise*, 1921

I heard two soldiers talking
  As they came down the hill—
The somber hill of Calvary,
  Bleak and black and still.
And one said, "The night is late;
  These thieves take long to die."
And one said, "I am sore afraid,
  And yet I know not why."

I heard two women weeping
  As down the hill they came.
And one was like a broken rose,
  One was like a flame.
And one said, "Now men shall rue
  This deed their hands have done."
And one said only through her tears,
  "My Son! My Son! My Son!"

I heard two angels singing
  Ere yet the dawn was bright,
And they were clad in shining robes,
  Robes and crowns of light.
And one sang, "Death is vanquished,"
  And one in golden voice
Sang, "Love hath conquered, conquered all;
  O Heaven and Earth, rejoice!"

# EASTER IS HERE

Margaret E. Jordan, published in *Type Lessons for Primary Teachers in the Study of Nature, Literature, and Art*, 1905

The lilies are white in the Easter light,
The lilies with hearts of gold.
And they silently tell,
With each milk-white bell,
The story an angel told.

And they whispered it long
To the weak and the strong,
To the rich and the poor among men;
Each Easter Day, till time dies away,
They will tell the tale again.

In the tomb new made
Where Christ was laid
An angel told the story
Of how He rose from death's repose,
The King of eternal glory.

## THE FLOWERS' SLEEP (FROM)
Annie Moore, published in *Werner's Readings and Recitations*, 1898

The little flowers come from the ground,
at Easter time, at Easter time;
They raise their heads and look around,
at happy Easter time.
And every little bud doth say:
"Be glad and full of joy today,
For all that sleeps shall wake again,
and spend a long, glad Easter day."

Then waken, sleeping butterflies,
at Easter time, at Easter time.
And spread your golden wings and rise,
at happy Easter time.
And these bright creatures seem to say:
"Be glad and full of joy today.
For all that sleeps shall wake again,
and spend a long, glad Easter day."

The happy birds come back again,
at Easter time, at Easter time;
The little streams awake and sing,
at happy Easter time.
And birds and streams together say:
"Be glad and full of joy today,
For all that sleeps shall wake again,
and spend a long, glad Easter day."

## COME TO JESUS

Father Frederick William Faber (1814-1863),
published in *Hymns Selected from
Frederick William Faber: Part 4*, 1900

Was there ever kindest shepherd
  Half so gentle, half so sweet,
As the Savior who would have us
Come and gather round His feet?

There's a wideness in God's mercy,
  Like the wideness of the sea;
There's a kindness in His justice,
  Which is more than liberty. . . .

There is welcome for the sinner
  And more graces for the good;
There is mercy with the savior;
There is healing in His Blood. . . .

But we make His love too narrow
  By false limits of our own
And we magnify His strictness
With a zeal He would not own. . . .

If our love were but more simple,
  We should take Him at His word;
And our lives would be all sunshine
  In the sweetness of our Lord.

## LOVING SHEPHERD OF THY SHEEP
## [ADAPTED]

Jane Elizabeth Leeson (1807-1882), published in
*Hymns and Scenes of Childhood,* 1842

Loving Shepherd of your sheep,

Keep your lamb, in safety keep;
Nothing can your power withstand,
None can pluck me from your hand. . . .

I would praise You every day,
Gladly all your will obey,
Like your blessed ones above
Happy in your precious love.

Loving Shepherd, ever near,
Teach your lamb your voice to hear,
Suffer not my steps to stray
From the straight and narrow way.

Where you lead me, I would go,
Walking in your steps below,
Till before my Father's throne
I shall know as I am known.

## THE ASCENSION

Sister Mary Josita Belger (1899-1978), published in
*Sing a Song of Holy Things*, 1945

Forty sunny days had passed
Since Jesus rose again.
The woods were full of singing birds,
And flowers were blooming then.
    And everything was still and sweet,
    The grass was soft and green.
    The Master stood upon the mount.
    His friends could all be seen.
Those loving friends stood all around
Wondering, for He said,
A little while and He would go
To heaven now instead.
    A little while to see Him,
    A little while at most;
    He was going to the Father,
    And would send the Holy Ghost.

They loved to hear Him call them "Friends."
They listened to His word.
And now their hearts were heavy,
At this sad thing they heard.
    But Jesus knew their broken hearts.
    "I will prepare a place,
    That where I go you, too, may come,
    And see Me face to face."
Then Jesus rose into the air,
Passing through a cloud.
They saw no more their Master;
In wonder, low they bowed. . . .

189

## THE COMING OF THE HOLY SPIRIT
Sister Mary Josita Belger (1899-1978), published in
*Sing a Song of Holy Things*, 1945

When Jesus stood upon the mount
With all His friends nearby,
He promised them that He would send
The Spirit from on high.

And so they prayed from day to day,
Until the time came near.
Mother Mary stayed with them
To keep away all fear.

Suddenly a mighty wind
Blew through the holy place
Where the apostles knelt to pray.
It filled each tiny space.

They saw a tongue of fire rest
Right over every head.
And no one talked just like himself,
But other ways instead.

The Holy Ghost had filled each heart,
Made each a soldier brave.
They went forth now to preach and teach,
And many souls to save.

## TRADITION
John B. Tabb (1845-1909), published in
*Child Verse*, 1899

WHEN home our blessed Lord was gone,

His mother lived alone with John;
For each had secrets to impart
That Love had taught them both by heart.


## SWEET MOTHER OF JESUS
Clementia (Sr. Mary Edward Feehan, 1878-????),
published in *The Cathedral Readers: Book 3*, 1920

Sweet Mother of Jesus

And my Mother too,
Teach me and help me
To love Him and you.

## THE BLESSED TRINITY

Sister Mary Josita Belger (1899-1978), published in
*Sing a Song of Holy Things*, 1945

God is one in Persons three—
Father, Son, and Spirit.
I do not know how it can be,
Even though I hear it.

But I believe it just the same,
And call the Persons three
By that all holy Name of names,
The Blessed Trinity.

God the Father gave His Son
To save the world from sin,
And God the Holy Ghost is Love,
And seeks our souls to win.

So when I make the holy cross
Before my prayers, you see,
I show that I believe that God
Is one in Persons three.

# THE RANN OF THE THREE
### Traditional Irish Prayer

Three folds in my garment,
Yet only one garment I bear.
Three joints in a finger,
Yet only one finger is there.
Three leaves in a shamrock,
Yet only one shamrock I wear.
Frost, ice, and snow,
These three are nothing but water.
Three Persons in God,
Yet only one God is there.

## *ANIMA CHRISTI*
## (SOUL OF CHRIST)

Traditional 14th-Century prayer, translated by
Cardinal John Henry Newman (1801-1890)

Soul of Christ, be my sanctification;
Body of Christ, be my salvation;
Blood of Christ, fill all my veins;
Water of Christ's side, wash out my stains;
Passion of Christ, my comfort be;
O good Jesus, listen to me;
In Thy wounds I fain* would hide;
Ne'er to be parted from Thy side;
Guard me, should the foe assail me;
Call me when my life shall fail me;
Bid me come to Thee above,
With Thy saints to sing Thy love,
World without end.
Amen.

* gladly; with pleasure

## THE SACRED HEART OF JESUS
Sister Mary Josita Belger (1899-1978), published in
*Sing a Song of Holy Things*, 1945

At night when all were sleeping
Within the convent walls,
Sister Margaret Mary rose,
And tiptoed through the halls.

Until she reached the chapel room
With dim red light aflame.
There she knelt in holy peace,
And whispered Jesus' Name.

One night when she was kneeling there,
She gave a little start,
For on the altar Jesus stood,
Showing His Sacred Heart.

He told her that He wished
His Sacred Heart were better known,
That He'd bless the homes where pictures
Of that loving Heart were shown.

He complained about the sinful world,
The cold, hard hearts of men,
And He promised help to sinners
Who would turn to Him again.

Through all the days of all her years,
Through every smallest part,
She tried to win this sinful world
For Jesus' Sacred Heart.

# TO THE IMMACULATE HEART OF MARY
### Janet P. McKenzie

Apart from the heart of Jesus
What heart has felt such pain
As the heart of Mother Mary,
Heart free of sin and stain.

Heart so pure, heart so bright,
Heart unlike all other;
Heart so clean, heart so white,
Heart of our Blessed Mother.

Heart of Immaculate Mary,
Heart pierced by grief and sword,
Convert my heart; incline my heart
To the Heart of our Lord.

Heart made pure, heart made bright,
Heart made like the Other;
Heart made clean, heart made white,
Heart like our Blessed Mother.

Heart that venerates—
My heart a still sanctuary.
Heart that consecrates—
My heart to Jesus through Mary.

# FIRST FRIDAY AND FIRST SATURDAY MEDITATIONS

## IN JESUS
### Annie Johnson Flint (1866-1933)

In the world, tribulation; but in Jesus—peace;
The heart of the whirlwind where its roarings cease,
A little home waiting, still and light and warm,
A safe sanctuary from the night and storm.

In the world, tribulation; but in Jesus—rest;
A sure place of refuge for the sore-opprest,
A guarded pavilion no device can take,
A strong-walled fortress no assault can shake. . . .

In the world, tribulation; but in Jesus—peace;
A deep, quiet harbor where the high waves cease,
A long-desired haven on a friendly shore,
Where the wild winds of oceans sweep the soul no more.

In the world, tribulation, trials all around,
For on earth no resting and no joys are found;
Let us flee to Jesus where all sorrows cease;
Here alone is gladness; here alone is peace.

## MY JESUS! MERCY!

Sister Mary Josita Belger (1899-1978), published in
*Sing a Song of Holy Things*, 1945

Dear Jesus, oh, how sad You were
The night before You died—
To think of leaving all Your friends
Without their Lord and Guide.

You knew as only God could know
The thoughts in Judas' heart.
You loved him still, and longed to see
His great, bad sins depart.

You called him "Friend," and loving looks
You gave through sad, sad eyes
On thinking of Your coming death,
That such poor souls might rise.

I cannot see how such a man
Did not fall down and cry,
To see his Master suffering so,
And know the reason why.

I think he was so bad, and yet
I do the very same
When I add sin to sin each day
Without a thought of shame.

Oh, Jesus, here before Your feet,
I lovingly adore.
Oh, help me now to keep my word,
And never hurt You more.

## THE HAUL OF FISH

T. V. Nicholas, published in *Gospel Rhymes*, 1947

Once Jesus told St. Peter,—they were in his
  fishing craft,—
To launch into the deep and let his nets down for a
  draught*;
St. Peter said they'd worked all night and taken
  nothing yet,
"But at Thy Word," he told Our Lord, "I will let down
  the net.
He let it down, and instantly got all his heart could
  wish,
The fishing-net was broken by the lovely load of fish.
He called his friends to help him from another little
  boat;
They heaped up fish in both till they could hardly
  keep afloat.

*Dear Lord, it's sometimes rather hard to try again*
  *and yet*
*You often mean to help us when You say: Let down*
  *the net:*
*So I'll copy great St. Peter, who had no success at all,*
*But at Your Word he tried again and got a splendid*
  *haul.*


* a draw; a pull through the water

## THE HELPER

Rev Hugh F. Blunt (1877-1957), published in
*Religious Poems for Little Folks*, 1936

My crown of thorns is great and strong
My scourging cords are think and long,
My cross is monstrous high and wide;
What matter? God is at my side.

## THE PRODIGAL SON
T. V. Nicholas, published in *Gospel Rhymes*, 1947

To welcome home the prodigal, his father made a feast,
The elder brother saw it and he sulked and said, "At least
You might have cooked a kid one day for me, your faithful
son,
You've killed fatted calf for *him*—and look at all he's
done."
The father begged him join the feast and bade him not
repine*,
"Son, thou art with me always and all I have is thine,"
You told him too of joyful thoughts this boy's return had
stirred,—
I think the prodigal was near reflecting as he heard:—

"It won't be very easy now for me to settle down,
For I've roamed around the country and I've knocked
about the town;
I feared my father's anger yet I've found his love increased.
But it's different in my father's house, yes, even when
they feast.

"Yet though it must seem strange at first I'll gladly make
my choice,
I'll stay for good,—and then one day I'll hear my father's
voice;
No longer words of welcome or of feasting shall be mine,
But 'Thou art with me always, son, and all I have is thine."


* pout; be unhappy

# THE WAY OF THE CROSS
Eleanor C. Donnelly (1838-1917), published in
*A Tuscan Magdalen*, 1896

I opened the Blessed Book
In the hush of a sylvan* spot,
And I read: "Whoever follows Me,
In darkness he walks not. . . . "

But a wind the woodland fann'd,
And the leaves of the forest shook,
Turning, as if with a viewless hand,
The leaves of that precious Book.

And lo! On another page,
I read again, with a sigh:
"If any man will come after Me,
Let him, himself, deny. . . .

O truth of truths! On the moss,
I knelt in the greenwood lone,
And pondered the secret of the Cross,
In the living Word made known. . . .

The way is narrow and rough,
Sharp stones the footpath strew,
And after the bleeding, burden'd Christ,
The suff'ring Christians go.

But a glow and a glory bright
On those pilgrims ever beam;
For the way of the Cross is the way of light,
Of light and love supreme!

* wooded; in the forest

# ADDITIONAL
# RESOURCES

## THE READING MOTHER (FROM)
Strickland Gillilan (1869-1954), written in 1892

I had a mother who read me things
That wholesome life to the boy-heart brings—
    Stories that stir with an upward touch,
    O, that each mother of boys were such.
    You may have tangible wealth untold,
    Caskets of jewels and coffers of gold.
    Richer than I you can never be—
    I had a mother who read to me.

# RECOMMENDED SPRING PICTURE BOOKS

## STELLAR CHOICES

★Davies, Nicola. *Outside Your Window: A First Book of Nature* – This book has poems and observations for each of the seasons of the year with bright illustrations that encourage children to explore and discover more about the wonder of the outdoors.

★Ets, Marie Hall. *Play with Me* – In this Caldecott Honor book, a little girl learns how to play with the insects and animals of the meadow.

★Mackall, Dandi. *The Story of the Easter Robin* – A little girl watches over a robin's nest as Easter draws near and learns lessons about Jesus and the Creator.

★Yolen, Jane and Andrew Fusck Peters. *Here's a Little Poem: A Very First Book of Poetry* – Containing more than sixty poems, this book for young children has cute and quirky illustrations.

## HOLIDAY AND RELIGIOUS BOOKS

Alexander, Sue. *Behold the Trees* – A unique picture-story of the trees of Israel, this beautiful book holds a special message of the value of trees for older readers—a special message for Arbor Day.

Bosco, Annette. *The Jesus Garden: An Easter Legend* – A sweet Easter story about the trees, flowers, and birds of the Garden of Gethsemane and how they were rewarded for their compassion for Jesus during His agony and death.

dePaoli, Tomie. *Mary, The Mother of Jesus* – This nicely illustrated book covers many events in the life of the Blessed Virgin including many of the mysteries of the rosary.

Guadagno, Geraldne and Maria Cristina lo Cascio. *St. Joseph's Story* – This well-written, beautifully illustrated book tells the quiet story of the carpenter who was the foster-father of Jesus.

Gurley, Nan. *Little Rose of Sharon* – In this Lenten parable, the little rose finds the Creator's great love for her as she sacrifices all she has for another.

Hunt, Angela Elwell. *The Tale of Three Trees* – In this traditional folktale, three trees all play an important role in the life of our King and Savior.

Jones, Jessie Orton. *Small Rain: Verses from the Bible* – A Caldecott Honor book, these selections are taken mostly from the Book of Psalms and are accompanied with cute illustrations.

Laughlin, Michael. *The Thornbush* – This is the story of the neglected thorn bush that provided the crown of thorns for Jesus on Good Friday.

Nobisso, Josephine. *The Weight of a Mass: A Tale of Faith* – What is the true value of a single Mass?

Politi, Leo. *Song of the Swallows* – This is the story of how a little boy prepares for the return of the swallows in San Juan Capistrano each year for St. Joseph's day on March 19.

Wildsmith, Brian. *The Easter Story* – Beginning with Palm Sunday, Jesus' donkey follows Him through all the events of Holy Week in this accurately chronicled and interesting account.

## DETECTING GOD IN NATURE
## (NATURE DETECTIVE)

Anthony, Joseph. *The Dandelion Seed* – Depicts the life cycle of a dandelion seed

Baylor, Byrd. *I'm in Charge of Celebrations* – As we experience the unique natures of so much of the outdoor life, we participate in the special events that often surround us, events that, sadly, many people miss. What special experiences and memories of God's creation can you recall and celebrate each year?

Bjork, Christina. *Linnea's Almanac* – This charming children's almanac contains birds, plants, and activities for each month of the year.

Krauss, Ruth. *The Happy Day* – In this Caldecott Honor book with simple text, the animals of the forest joyfully greet spring.

Lindbergh, Reeve. *North Country Spring* – Short poems call each animal and plant to spring out.

Lloyd, Megan Wagner. *Finding Wild* – With bright water-color illustrations, this short, sweet book helps everyone (country or city) to find wild nature.

Schnur, Steven. *Spring: An Alphabet Acrostic* – Twenty-six short poems, with bright illustrations, depict many aspects of the spring season.

Schnur. Steven. *Spring Thaw* – The magic of a new season shines through this brightly illustrated book.

Tudor, Tasha. *Springs of Joy* – With Tasha Tudor's glorious illustrations, this book is a "statement of delight" and cause for joy itself.

Winer, Yvonne. *Birds Build Nests* – Including detailed illustrations, the how, when, where, and why questions of birds' nests are answered here in verse.

# INSPECTING GOD'S GLORIOUS CREATION (NATURALIST)

Arnosky, Jim. *Crinkleroot's Book of Animal Tracking* – In this lively and informative introduction to the art of animal tracking, Crinkleroot shares his knowledge and secrets, including his own helpful wildlife charts.

Aston, Dianna. *An Egg Is Quiet* – A gorgeous and educational introduction to over sixty different types of eggs, this book paints a beautiful picture of the various characteristics of eggs.

Boring, Mel and Diane Burns and Leslie Dendy. *Fun with Nature: Take-Along Guide* – Full of colorful illustrations and plenty of facts, these guides to many aspects of nature (butterflies, salamanders, trees, frogs, squirrels, animals tracks and much more) help with identification and provide hands-on activities as well as space for sketches and notes.

Boring, Mel and Diane Burns and Laura Evert. *More Fun with Nature: Take-Along Guide* – Five guides to nature in one, this book covers topics such as wildflowers, berries, nuts, birds, seashells, and rocks.

Davies, Nicola. *A Butterfly Is Patient* – Gorgeous and informative, this book is an excellent introduction to butterflies in all their beauty and wonder.

Fox, Paula. *Traces* – In this book, we learn how to more carefully observe and interpret the sights and sounds of nature.

## RESPECTING GOD'S CREATION
## (ECO-CATHOLIC)

Brown, Peter. *The Curious Garden* – Through the efforts of one, small, determined boy, one small, neglected garden grows throughout the city.

Burleigh, Robert. *Into the Woods: John James Audubon Lives His Dream* – Beautifully illustrated, this short biography emphasizes Audubon's love of nature and his obsession to paint the many, various species of birds.

Burton, Virginia. *The Little House* – The story of a little country house that got caught up in urban sprawl, this classic story helps us understand that sometimes our connection with nature is easier outside the city.

Cole, Henry. *On Meadowview Street* – Caroline, bit by bit, converts her yard into a meadow.

Davies, Jacqueline. *The Boy Who Drew Birds: A Story of John James Audubon* – Learn more about this wildlife artist, how he befriended birds, and what he did to fuel his curiosity about bird migration.

Kooser, Ted. *Bag in the Wind* – Interesting illustrations help tell the story of a discarded bag as it blows around the neighborhood. We've all seen them; how many of us stop to pick them up and consider what their story may be?

## REFLECTING ON THE MYSTERY OF GOD
## (MYSTIC)

Archer, Micha. *Daniel Finds a Poem* – What do the animals in the park think poetry is? What do you think poetry is? What would be your quiet poem?

Bunting, Eve. *Secret Place* – Through this book, Eve Bunting encourages us to find secret places nearby, peaceful places where wild things live and grow.

Lemniscates. *Silence* – Turn off the noise; listen. Go outside; listen. Can you hear God?

Martin, Bill Jr. and John Archambault. *Listen to the Rain* – A lyrical book that evokes the sound and silence of rain in perfect meter with illustrations that enhance the gentle text

Sweetland, Nancy. *God's Quiet Things* – God's silent creation surrounds us. This short, sweet book encourages us to observe, to listen, to see God's hand in all of nature.

## GENERAL NATURE BOOKS

Bauer, Marion Dane. *In Like a Lion* – March is personified as both a lion and a lamb in this amusing tale.

Berenstain, Stan and Jan. *The Berenstain Bear's Four Seasons* – A short, poetic introduction to the four seasons

Bjork, Christina. *Linnea's Windowsill Garden* – Informative and inspiring as a beginning indoor gardening book, Linnea teaches us how to grow (and take care of) plants from seed and plants from pits.

Florian, Douglas. *Handsprings* – These short poems capture the freshness and promise of spring and are accompanied by quirky, humorous illustrations.

Hamerstrom, Frances. *Walk When the Moon Is Full* – Each month, during the full moon, a walk through the night is described and accompanied by detailed black-and-white pictures.

Holling, Holling C. *Paddle-to-the-Sea* – An Indian boy carves a wooden canoe with a figure in it and sets it on a melting riverbank north of Lake Superior so it can begin its journey to the Atlantic Ocean. Follow its journey.

Locker, Thomas. *Water Dance* – Describes and attractively illustrates rivers, waterfalls, lakes and other water forms while teaching about the water cycle

Manning, Mick and Brita Granström. *Wild Adventures* – Discover the wonder of nature using the varied outdoor activities in this fun, educational book. The adventures of nature await!

Paul, Miranda. *Water Is Water* – With simple rhythmic text and brilliant paintings, the various forms water can take are examined.

Salas, Laura Purdie. *Water Can Be* – This is a poetic exploration of what water can be throughout the seasons.

Southwell, Jandelyn. *Little Country Town* – In gentle verse, twilight comes to a little country town.

Stevenson, Robert L. and Tasha Tudor. *A Child's Garden of Verses* – This collection of sixty-six of Robert Lewis Stevenson's poems is illustrated in the watercolors of Tasha Tudor.

Updike, John. *A Child's Calendar* – Another Caldecott Honor book, this one gives us poems and pictures for each month of the year beautifully illustrated in the watercolors of Trina Schart Hyman.

Wallner, Alexandra. *Beatrix Potter* – The poetical and artistic gifts of Beatrix Potter are revealed in this sensitive biographical picture book. How did her short animal tales, through which her love of nature shines through, come to be written?

Ward, Jennifer. *The Busy* Tree – With rhyming text and bright illustrations, this short book describes the many and varied activities that evolve around one oak tree.

Winter, Jeanette. *Emily Dickinson's Letters to the World* – This gentle introduction to the life and poetry of Emily Dickinson is full of vibrant paintings.

Yolen, Jane. *The Emily Sonnets: The Life of Emily Dickinson in Verse* – A poetic and inspiring rendition of Emily Dickinson's life and poetry for older children and adults.

## CHILDREN'S NATURE AUTHORS

The following authors of children's books often have many elements of nature in their writings:

Arnosky, Jim
Barker, Cicely Mary (Flower Fairies)
Brink, Carol Ryrie
Burgess, Thornton (any and all)
Campbell, Sam (especially the Living Forest series)
Erdrich, Louise
George, Jean Craighead
Hiaagen, Carl (especially his environmental series:
    *Hoot, Flush, Scat,* and *Chomp*)
Holling, Holling C.
Kjelgaard, Jim
Montgomery, Lucy Maud
O'Dell, Scott
Paulsen, Gary
Pellowski, Anne (Latsch Valley Farm series)
Ransome, Arthur
Whelan, Gloria
Wilder, Laura Ingalls

# RECOMMENDED ADULT RESOURCES

The following lists of books are intended to aid you in becoming more confident as a nature mentor and student of natural history. This subject used to be taught in schools along with reading, writing, and 'rithmetic. In addition, years ago people were more connected to nature through farming, gardening, and general rural living. Scott Sampson states, "By the close of the 1900s, most Americans could describe themselves as naturalists" (*How to Raise a Wild Child*). Browse through the lists and pick at least one book from each category to educate and inspire you. Most books can be found in your local library or purchased new or used online.

The "Why" of Nature

- *Last Child in the Woods: Saving Our Children from Nature-Deficit Disorder* by Richard Louv
- *Step into Nature: Nurturing Imagination and Spirit in Everyday Life* by Patrice Vecchione
- *The Joyful Mystery: Field Notes toward a Green Thomism* by Christopher J. Thompson
- *The Nature Fix: Why Nature Makes Us Happier, Healthier, and More Creative* by Florence Williams

Connection with Nature

- *A Blessing of Toads: A Guide to Living with Nature* by Sharon Lovejoy
- *How to Be a Wildflower: A Field Guide* by Katie Daisy
- *The Curious Nature Guide: Explore the Natural Wonders All Around You* by Clare Walker Leslie
- *The Secret Wisdom of Nature: Trees, Animals, and the Extraordinary Balance of All Living Things* by Peter Wohlleben

📖 *What the Robin Knows: How Birds Reveal the Secrets of the Natural World* by Jon Young

Nature Activity Books—Outdoor Adventuring

📖 *15 Minutes Outside: 365 Ways to Get Out of the House and Connect with Your Kids* by Rebecca P. Cohen [elementary age]

📖 *Go Wild! 101 Things to Do Outdoors before You Grow Up* by Jo Schofield and Fiona Danks [teens]

📖 *Hands-On Nature: Information and Activities for Exploring the Environment with Children* by Jenepher Lingelbach [Grades K-6]

📖 *I Love Dirt: 52 Activities to Help You and Your Kids Discover the Wonders of Nature* by Jennifer Ward [ages 4-8]

📖 *Roots, Shoots, Buckets & Boots: Gardening Together with Children* by Sharon Lovejoy

📖 *Teaching Kids to Love the Earth: Sharing a Sense of Wonder . . . 186 Outdoor Activities for Parents and Other Teachers* by Herman, Passineau, Schimpf, & Treuer [all ages]

📖 *The Boy's Book of Adventure: The Little Guidebook for Smart and Resourceful Boys* by Michele Lecreux [for girls too!]

📖 *The Wild Weather Book: Loads of Things to Do Outdoors in Rain, Wind and Snow* by Fiona Danks and Jo Schofield

📖 *Vitamin N: The Essential Guide to a Nature-Rich Life—500 Ways to Enrich the Health & Happiness of Your Family & Community* by Richard Louv

Nature Journaling

📖 *Drawn to Nature through the Journals of Clare Walker Leslie*

📖 *Keeping a Nature Journal: Discover a Whole New Way of Seeing the World Around You* by Clare Walker Leslie & Charles E. Roth [ideas and "how to"]

📖 *Nature Journal: A Guided Journal for Illustrating and Recording Your Observations of the Natural World* with Clare Walker Leslie

📖 *The Country Diary of an Edwardian Lady* by Edith Holden

📖 *The Naturalist's Notebook for Tracking Changes in the Natural World Around You* by Nathaniel T. Wheelwright & Bernd Heinrich

Nature Crafts and Drawing Books

📖 *Crafting with Nature: Grow or Gather Your Own Supplies for Simple Handmade Crafts, Gifts & Recipes* by Amy Renea

📖 *Make It Wild: 101 Things to Make and Do Outdoors* by Fiona Danks and Jo Schofield

📖 *Nature Crafts for Kids: 50 Fantastic Things to Make with Mother Nature's Help* by Gwen Diehn & Terry Krautwurst

📖 *Peggy Dean's Guide to Nature Drawing and Watercolor: Learn to Sketch, Ink, and Paint Flowers, Plants, Trees, and Animals* by Peggy Dean

Nature Books for Grandparents

📖 *Granny Camp by Sharon Lovejoy*

📖 *The Rhythm of Family: Discovering a Sense of Wonder through the Seasons* by Amanda Blake Soule with Stephen Soule

📖 *Toad Cottages & Shooting Stars: Grandma's Bag of Tricks* by Sharon Lovejoy

The Practice of *Shinrin-yoku:* Forest Therapy or Forest Bathing

- 📖 *Your Guide to Forest Bathing: Experience the Healing Power of Nature* by M. Amos Clifford
- 📖 Review the teaching philosophies of educators such as Maria Montessori and Charlotte Mason

The Practice of Mindfulness

- 📖 *A Catholic Guide to Mindfulness* by Susan Brinkmann, OCDS
- 📖 *The Mindful Catholic: Finding God One Moment at a Time* by Dr Gregory Bottaro
- 📖 *The Practice of the Presence of God* by Br. Lawrence of the Resurrection
- 📖 *The Sacrament of the Present Moment* by Jean-Pierre de Caussade (also published as *Abandonment to Divine Providence*)

---

"For if they so far succeeded in knowledge that they could speculate about the world, how did they not more quickly find its Lord?"

Wisdom 13:9

---

# APPENDIX

# SEEKING GOD IN NATURE WITH THE CHURCH

# ASSURANCES AND GENERAL COUNSELS: SEEKING GOD IN NATURE VS. NATURE WORSHIP

With the advent of the New Age Movement or New Age Spirituality, many Catholics have become rightfully cautious regarding seeking God (and praying with Him) in nature as this book series promotes. In order to reassure you and provide some general counsel and advice, the following "lessons" are provided regarding the proper place the reverence of God has in His creation and the appropriateness of communing with Him in the natural world. Below are various appropriate passages from the *Catechism of the Catholic Church*, papal documents, and teachings of the United States bishops. By following the guidelines established with these various Church authorities, we can be assured not to go astray or to lead others down a questionable path of holiness.

Remember these basic principles when using the natural world to converse with God and advance in the life of prayer:

1. God is distinct from His creation. A tree is not God, but can help us better understand the attributes, love, and mercy of God.
2. While it is our intent to learn more about the natural world, this knowledge is for the sole purpose of uniting ourselves closer to the living God, the God of all creation.
3. There is nothing that exists that was not created by God—with a purpose. By understanding the uniqueness of each individual creation, its God-given purpose, and its connection to the rest of

creation, we can learn much about God and our relationship with Him and His creation.

4. God wants you to be surrounded with truth, beauty, and goodness. Creation gives us a glimpse of these features of God and fills us with gratitude.

5. The sole purpose of our existence is to unite our will perfectly with the Will of God and so attain perfect happiness in heaven. Any thing, any person, or any "method" or means of prayer that impedes our goal of uniting ourselves with the Triune God by increasing our self-centeredness or deflecting the reverence that belongs to God to any other person or object is not in accordance with divine teaching or the authority of the Catholic Church.

I promote communing with God in the natural world as it has worked unfailingly for me throughout my life— even as a professed Secular Carmelite. God speaks in eternal silence and in holy silence must be heard by the soul. This silence is often found in the stillness of the natural world. Matthew Kelly often speaks of spending time in the "classroom of silence." For me, nature provides the best classroom—free of the distractions of daily life.

If I spend too little time in silence with God in nature, my peace quickly evaporates, just as not frequenting the sacraments or spending too little time with Jesus in the Blessed Sacrament of the Altar does.

What drew me as a convert to the Catholic Church is the Church's vast array of available means to attain holiness. Perhaps this method of communing with the God of the universe will assist you—and your loved ones as well— along the path of holiness. That is my deep desire.

# A BRIEF LESSON ON NEW AGE SPIRITUALITY

While the gamut of New Age spirituality is vast and is composed of a variety of theologies, consider the following generally accepted principles of this philosophy: (Note that all of these are in conflict with the teachings of the Catholic Church.)

- No central authority or teaching, no formal doctrine, or membership
- Contains part of many "isms" such as Pantheism (All things are divine.), Gnosticism (salvation by knowledge), and occultism (knowledge or use of supernatural forces or beings)
- God and creation are one. There is no separation between them.
- Christ is a type of energy, not necessarily an individual being.
- Morality is individually determined—moral relativism
- Influenced by Eastern religions and forms of meditation
- Man is divine and perfected through reincarnation.

For our purposes, remember that God and creation are not one. Creation is a *reflection* of God and can help us come to know Him better. Knowledge of the natural world serves to draw us into closer union with the Creator as we come to see the diversity, beauty, and goodness of nature. We can become more deeply connected to God —and grow in gratitude for His constant presence and many gifts—when we see His hand in the world around us and can pray gratefully to Him in the silence of creation. We can join with all creation to sing praise to the glory of our loving God!

# LESSONS FROM THE *CATECHISM OF THE CATHOLIC CHURCH*

The following are excerpts from the *Catechism* regarding God and the natural (visible) world that should assure us that this path of union with God is trustworthy and in full communion with the Holy See:

¶32 . . . As St. Paul says of the Gentiles: For what can be known about God is plain to them, because God has shown it to them. Ever since the creation of the world his invisible nature, namely, his eternal power and deity, has been clearly perceived in the things that have been made (Rom 1:19-20; cf., Acts 14:15, 17; 17:27-28; Wis 13:1-9). And St. Augustine issues this challenge: Question the beauty of the earth, question the beauty of the sea, question the beauty of the air distending and diffusing itself, question the beauty of the sky . . . question all these realities. All respond: "See, we are beautiful." Their beauty is a profession [*confessio*]. These beauties are subject to change. Who made them if not the Beautiful One [Pulcher] who is not subject to change? (St. Augustine, *Sermo* 241, 2: Patrologia Latina 38, 1134)

¶41 All creatures bear a certain resemblance to God, most especially man, created in the image and likeness of God. The manifold perfections of creatures—their truth, their goodness, their beauty all reflect the infinite perfection of God. Consequently we can name God by taking his creatures' perfections as our starting point, "for from the greatness and beauty of created things comes a corresponding perception of their Creator" (Wisdom 13:5).

¶293 Scripture and Tradition never cease to teach and celebrate this fundamental truth: "The world was made for the glory of God" (*Dei Filius*, can. # 5: S 3025). St. Bonaventure explains that God created all things "not to increase his glory, but to show it forth and to communicate it" (St. Bonaventure, *In II Sent.* I, 2, 2, 1), for God has no other reason for creating than his love and goodness: "Creatures came into existence when the key of love opened his hand" (St. Thomas Aquinas, *Sent. II*, prol.). The First Vatican Council explains:

This one, true God, of his own goodness and "almighty power", not for increasing his own beatitude, nor for attaining his perfection, but in order to manifest this perfection through the benefits which he bestows on creatures, with absolute freedom of counsel "and from the beginning of time, made out of nothing both orders of creatures, the spiritual and the corporeal. . ." (13 *Dei Filius* I: DS 3002; cf Lateran Council IV (1215): DS 800.7)

¶294 The glory of God consists in the realization of this manifestation and communication of his goodness, for which the world was created. . . ."

GOD TRANSCENDS CREATION AND IS PRESENT TO IT
¶300 God is infinitely greater than all his works: "You have set your glory above the heavens" (Ps 8:1; cf. Sir 43:28). Indeed, God's "greatness is unsearchable" (Ps 145:3). But because he is the free and sovereign Creator, the first cause of all that exists, God is present to his creatures' inmost being: "In him we live and move and have our being" (Acts 17:28). In the words of St. Augustine, God is "higher than my highest and more inward than my innermost self" (St. Augustine, Conf: 3, 6, 11: PL 32, 688). God upholds and sustains creation.

¶337 God himself created the visible world in all its richness, diversity and order. . . . On the subject of creation, the sacred text teaches the truths revealed by God for our salvation (*Dei Verbum* Cf. 11), permitting us to "recognize the inner nature, the value and the ordering of the whole of creation to the praise of God" (*Lumen Gentium* 36 #2).

¶338 Nothing exists that does not owe its existence to God the Creator. . . .

¶339 Each creature possesses its own particular goodness and perfection. . . . Each of the various creatures, willed in its own being, reflects in its own way a ray of God's infinite wisdom and goodness. Man must therefore respect the particular goodness of every creature, to avoid any disordered use of things which would be in contempt of the Creator and would bring disastrous consequences for human beings and their environment.

¶340 God wills the interdependence of creatures: the sun and the moon, the cedar and the little flower, the eagle and the sparrow: the spectacle of their countless diversities and inequalities tells us that no creature is self-sufficient. Creatures exist only in dependence on each other, to complete each other, in the service of each other.

¶341 The beauty of the universe: the order and harmony of the created world results from the diversity of beings and from the relationships which exist among them. Man discovers them progressively as the laws of nature. They call forth the admiration of scholars. The beauty of creation reflects the infinite beauty of the Creator and ought to inspire the respect and submission of man's intellect and will.

¶344 There is a solidarity among all creatures arising from the fact that all have the same Creator and are all ordered to his glory . . .

¶2416 *Animals* are God's creatures. He surrounds them with his providential care. By their mere existence they bless him and give him glory (Cf. Mt 6:26; Dan 3:79-81). Thus men owe them kindness. We should recall the gentleness with which saints like St. Francis of Assisi or St. Philip Neri treated animals.

## LESSONS FROM RECENT PAPAL DOCUMENTS

One of the earliest papal documents to call attention to the environment is Pope Saint Paul VI's 1971 letter, *Octogesima Adveniens*, his reflection on the challenges of the post-industrial society. Here, he calls the environment a "wide-ranging social problem which concerns the entire human family" (¶21). Pope Saint John Paul II again addresses ecological matters in the 1988 *Sollicitudo Socialis (On Social Concern)*; and, in 1990, became the first pope to devote an entire papal document to the environmental issue: "Peace with God the Creator, Peace with All of Creation" (1990)—a document well worth reading. An entire chapter of *The Compendium of the Social Doctrine of the Church* (2004) addresses the topic of "Safeguarding the Environment." This chapter was condensed into "The Ten Commandments for the Environment" by Bishop Giampaolo Crepaldi in 2005.

Pope Benedict XVI spent so much of his papacy promoting an environmental message through addresses, encyclicals, and scientific conferences that he became known as the "Green Pope." Pope Francis has spoken frequently about ecological concerns and addressed his 2015 encyclical *Laudato Si': On Care for Our Common*

*Home* not just to a Catholic audience but to "every person living on this planet" (¶3).

For our purposes, however, let us limit our study to those papal references that especially address seeking and praising God in creation.

"PEACE WITH GOD THE CREATOR, PEACE WITH ALL OF CREATION" (Pope Saint John Paul II, 1990):

¶13 An education in ecological responsibility is urgent . . . The first educator, however, is the family, where the child learns to respect his neighbor and to love nature.

¶14 Finally, the aesthetic value of creation cannot be overlooked. Our very contact with nature has a deep restorative power; contemplation of its magnificence imparts peace and serenity. The Bible speaks again and again of the goodness and beauty of creation, which is called to glorify God . . .

¶16 It is my hope that the inspiration of Saint Francis will help us to keep ever alive a sense of "fraternity" with all those good and beautiful things which Almighty God has created. And may he remind us of our serious obligation to respect and watch over them with care, in light of that greater and higher fraternity that exists within the human family.

*COMPENDIUM OF THE SOCIAL DOCTRINE OF THE CHURCH* (2004):

*¶487 The attitude that must characterize the way man acts in relation to creation is essentially one of gratitude and appreciation; the world, in fact, reveals the mystery of God who created and sustains it.* If the relationship with God is placed aside, nature is stripped of its profound meaning and impoverished. If on the other hand,

nature is rediscovered in its creaturely dimension, channels of communication with it can be established, its rich and symbolic meaning can be understood, allowing us to enter into its realm of *mystery*. This realm opens the path of man to God, Creator of heaven and earth. *The world presents itself before man's eyes as evidence of God*, the place where his creative, providential and redemptive power unfolds.

*CARITAS IN VERITATE* (Pope Benedict XVI, 2009): ¶48 ". . . Nature speaks to us of the Creator (cf. Romans 1:20) and his love for humanity."

MEETING WITH PRIESTS AND DEACONS—August 6, 2008, Pope Benedict XVI: "If we observe what came into being around monasteries, how in those places small paradises, oases of creation were and continue to be born, it becomes evident that these were not only words. Rather, wher-ever the Creator's Word was properly understood, wher-ever life was lived with the redeeming Creator, people strove to save creation and not to destroy it."

*LAUDATO SI'* (Pope Francis, 2015):

¶85 "From panoramic vistas to the tiniest living form, nature is a constant source of wonder and awe. It is also a continuing revelation of the divine." . . . "To sense each creature singing the hymn of its existence is to live joyfully in God's love and hope." This contemplation of creation allows us to discover in each thing a teaching which God wishes to hand on to us, "for the believer, to contemplate creation is the hear a message, to listen to a paradoxical and silent voice."

¶87 When we can see God reflected in all that exists, our hearts are moved to praise the Lord for all his creatures and to worship him in union with them.

¶97 As he [Jesus] made his way throughout the land, he often stopped to contemplate the beauty sown by his Father, and invited his disciples to perceive a divine message in things . . .

¶233 The universe unfolds in God, who fills it completely. Hence, there is a mystical meaning to be found in a leaf, in a mountain trail, in a dewdrop, in a poor person's face. The ideal is not only to pass from the exterior to the interior to discover the action of God in the soul, but also to discover God in all things.

¶234 ". . . the mystic experiences the intimate connection between God and all beings, and thus feels that all things are God." Standing awestruck before a mountain, he or she cannot separate this experience from God, and perceives that the interior awe being lived has to be entrusted to the Lord . . .

¶246 . . . Teach us to discover the worth of each thing, to be filled with awe and contemplation, to recognize that we are profoundly united with every creature as we journey towards your infinite light.

## Lessons from the United States Conference of Catholic Bishops

In 1991, the United States Conference of Catholic Bishops published *Renewing the Earth: An Invitation to Reflection and Action on Environment in Light of Catholic Social Teaching,* and, in 2001, *Global Climate Change: A Plea for Dialogue, Prudence, and the Common Good.* Let us examine some excerpts from the former document.

For many people, the environmental movement has reawakened appreciation of the truth that, through the created gifts of nature, men and women encounter their

Creator. The Christian vision of a sacramental universe —a world that discloses the Creator's presence by visible and tangible signs—can contribute to making the earth a home for the human family once again. Pope John Paul II has called for Christians to respect and protect the environment, so that through nature people can "contemplate the mystery of the greatness and love of God. . . . Dwelling in the presence of God, we begin to experience ourselves as part of creation, as stewards within it, not separate from it. As faithful stewards, fullness of life comes from living responsibly within God's creation (III-A).

Nature shares in God's goodness, and contemplation of its beauty and richness raised our hearts and minds to God. . . . Through the centuries, Catholic theologians and philosophers, like St. Paul before them, continue to search for God in reasoning about the created world (IV-A).

We remind *parents* that they are the first and principal teachers of children. It is from parents that children will learn love of the earth and delight in nature. It is at home that they develop the habits of self-control, concern, and care that lie at the heart of environmental morality (V-B).

## TWO CURRENT PRACTICES

Seeking God and communing with Him in nature raises several potential "red flags" regarding two currently popular practices: the Japanese practice of *shinrin-yoku*, or forest therapy (forest bathing) and mindfulness.

Many scientific studies show that spending time in nature can have a positive effect on us physically, emotionally, and spiritually. Forest therapy, a concept practiced instinctively for eons, has fallen from practice in modern times. Spending refreshing periods of time with God in the natural world can be spiritually empowering. Organized "immersions" are becoming popular. Be cautious and aware, ensuring that the focus centers on God the Creator—source of all existence.

Mindfulness, derived from a Buddhist meditation technique, also has the potential to lead a Catholic astray. Although similar to the accepted Catholic practices of the Practice of the Presence of God and the Sacrament of the Present Moment, Buddhist mindfulness is centered on the mind; Catholic meditation always centers on God. We want to treasure each moment with God in the natural world, but only in a way that leads us directly to Him.

Educate yourself regarding these two practices by reading one or more of the resources suggested in the Appendix, or research these practices online.

---

As we deepen our connection with nature—and therefore with our loving God—let us try to develop a "sacramental imagination." According to Mary C. Boys, this is a "vision that sees all creation as mediating the divine." This vision may be easier for children than adults. To seek God through His creation, search for His reflection —consider what each creation can teach us about God, and embrace each gift of nature as a continuation of the mystery that is God: "Even when he reveals himself, God remains a mystery beyond words: 'If you understood him, it would not be God'" *(CCC* ¶230 quoting St. Augustine).

Immerse yourself in nature. Ponder in holy silence His wondrous creation. In all things, give Him glory. Give thanks.